OUR DIVINE MANDATE

Completing Humanity's Great Commission

By: Tom Casey

Author of:

Studies in The Kingdom of God

Copyright: 2020

All rights reserved

ISBN: 978-0-9984514-2-8

To Andrea,

Thank you for giving me the time,
space and your keen eye in the writing of this book;
knowing that it will not be the last.
I have witnessed your love, yet again.
I love you and could not have done this without you.

TABLE OF CONTENTS

ENDORSEMENTS

FOREWORD

INTRODUCTION

AUTHOR'S NOTE

1) *Our Mandate: God Shares His Earthly Rule*   14

2) *Delayed But Not Disqualified*   25

3) *God's Eternal Devotion To Humanity: The Blood Covenant*   30

4) *Spiritual Realities Prophetically Present*   48

5) *Fixing Our Eyes And Following Our Example*   63

6) *Image Bearers Equipped, Trained And Mentored By God*   81

7) *But The People Who Know Their God*   124

8) *Regents Resurrected, Ruling & Subduing The Earth*   147

9) *Our Mandate Completed*   161

Moving Forward – What Is Next?   187

About The Author

ENDORSEMENTS

"In our pursuit of understanding the Jesus of the Church, we have lost touch with the God of Creation. Tom Casey has done a brilliant job of reacquainting us with YHWH, as the Hebrews called Him, and His original mission and mandate for humanity."

Bob Scott – CEO, Joseph Company Global

"Tom Casey's new book, *Our Divine Mandate*, is a compelling clarion call to all Christians not to be complacent in these Last Days. Unfortunately, most Christians do not appreciate the larger plan of God, and they tend to focus entirely on the Great Commission in Matthew 28. They neglect that the "first commission," which Tom refers to as the Divine Mandate, was issued in Genesis 1:28 and has never been nullified. This Divine Mandate ("Be fruitful and increase in number; fill the earth and subdue it. Rule over the fish in the sea and the birds in the sky and over every living creature that moves on the ground.") is the focus of both God's creation and His restoration.

Tom emphasizes that we are not just created beings, but "representatives and regents" of God on the earth, as Adam and Eve were. But we will succeed where Adam and Eve failed. And Tom gives us a clear vision of the rights and responsibilities of that role. Further, Tom explains the process that God has used to restore us to the role as regents of the earth, including the training and discipleship process needed to prepare humanity for this amazing opportunity, enabled by the Holy Spirit and with Jesus as our role model of the perfect regent to emulate! Tom also explains how Satan has been so adamant in his attempts to undermine this restoration process.

Many Christians are just waiting for the return of Jesus and to receive their "heavenly reward" and fail to realize that the true destiny of human beings is, and has always been, to rule (subdue) the earth. Tom stresses the importance of using our remaining time in this life to prepare for the future that God planned for us from the beginning. Tom's description of Christ's return, His final victory, and redeemed humanity taking our rightful place as regents on the earth during the Millennium and on the new earth in the New Jerusalem, is awe-inspiring. What an amazing future we have to look forward to, and how fortunate we are that Tom Casey spells out God's plan so clearly. This book is a must-read!"

Dr. Dean R. Spitzer, internationally-acclaimed author, researcher, scholar, and Bible college professor

FOREWORD

I have known the author, Tom Casey, for nearly fifty years. We were friends in high school and when I became a youth pastor in St. Louis, in our early twenties, Tom also moved there to be part of the youth ministry before embarking on his business career. Tom has excelled in the business world—working in management for companies like Toshiba America and IBM. In addition, he has been involved with starting two technology companies.

I agreed to write this Foreword because of my long friendship with Tom and because he has acquired understanding and experience that I believe can benefit the followers of Jesus. In Tom's first book, *"Studies In The Kingdom of God,"* he explains what the Kingdom of God is and how each person can experience it by responding to personal "invitations" from the Lord.

I am assured from the Scriptures that the Lord's commitment is to release a spirit of revival on the body of Christ across the nations. This will happen within the context of seeing her identity as Jesus' cherished Bride, and will transform her to such a degree that she will one day be without spot or wrinkle. He is doing this one person at a time. We must not lose sight of this aspect of His mighty plans for His Kingdom.

In this, his second book, *"Our Divine Mandate"*, Tom emphasizes this fact. He reminds us that the Lord's original commission to the human race is to multiply and fill the earth, rule over it, and subdue it as God's regents. Even though Adam and Eve rebelled against God in the Garden of Eden, this mandate wasn't voided and it hasn't changed. As a result, through Christ, the Father has been calling His people to this original place of function and authority. As God has been working to accomplish this, He has done so one person, one people group and one generation at a time.

As Tom says in the book, God is not only restoring humanity to their rightful place as His regents, He is revealing Himself to us and training us in what it means to be His prophetic people, covenant partners, and image-bearers within the established order of the Kingdom of God. This training has been going on in a very deliberate way for many generations. God will continue this restoration until the end of this age and into Jesus' millennial reign.

We see His pattern and plan by considering what He did in bringing Israel out Egypt and through the wilderness. During this time, God revealed Himself to them and trained them in His Kingdom realities and prophetic activities for 40 years. Eventually, God brought them into the land He promised them and led them to fulfill aspects of His eternal purposes.

The Lord's training of the body of Christ to fulfill His mandate for the human race has many parallels to how He led and trained the children of Israel to possess their land of promise. The Lord's people have a mandate to pursue, a restoration process to undergo, and a Kingdom training to engage with. It involves getting to know our covenant God, the nature of our relationship with Him, His divine activities, and the ministry and leadership of the Holy Spirit. Just like God's people in the wilderness, we have much to learn as individuals and as a faith community. This is the focus of Tom's book—to call and equip people to walk in the realities of the Kingdom of God. I believe you will be inspired and strengthened by Tom's book.

Mike Bickle - International House of Prayer of Kansas City

INTRODUCTION

The scriptures clearly identify a mandate, a great commission, being assigned to all of humanity by God, in Genesis chapters 1 and 2.

Before we begin, I want to clarify two things: 1) A mandate is, simply, *"an official order or commission to do something."*[1] 2) Theologians throughout the centuries have attached the term "the Great Commission" to Jesus' command to His disciples, in Matthew 28, before He returned to heaven after His resurrection. This command is for the followers of Jesus to go and proclaim the good news of the Kingdom of God (the gospel) to all nations, in every generation. Neither Jesus nor any of the New Testament writers ever refer to this mandate as "the Great Commission". It is a relatively modern theological term that has been adopted to emphasize its importance to Jesus' disciples.

With this being said, humanity's original great commission is very simply stated by God in Genesis:

> *"Then God said, "Let Us make man in Our image, according to Our likeness; and let them rule over the fish of the sea and over the birds of the sky and over the cattle and over all the earth, and over every creeping thing that creeps on the earth." "God blessed them; and God said to them, "Be fruitful and multiply, and fill the earth, and subdue it."*
> Genesis 1:26, 28 NASB

The purpose of this book is to present and explain that this original command from God has always been and continues to be humanity's true "marching orders". God has completely devoted Himself and His Kingdom resources and activities to see humanity complete this commission. In this book we will see that God has put in place, from the very beginning, a very practical and engaging plan for preparing every individual and faith community to equip, train and mentor us, to this end. The Holy Spirit desires to engage each

---

[1] Dictionary.com

of us in the spiritual activities He will use to eventually bring this reality to pass. This is the focus of God's attention in this generation. You will see how to recognize and embrace God's invitation to join Him in His Kingdom activities, and to move forward with Him toward the completion of this commission.

It is important for us to understand that this original mandate in Genesis and the command Jesus gave His disciples at His ascension are intricately related. In fact, the commission Jesus gave His disciples is more of a continuation of the original order God gave humanity. Both are focused on the activities of human beings to declare the reality and presence of the Kingdom of God, and to powerfully represent and demonstrate its presence throughout the earth. As we will see, even Jesus, Himself, *proclaimed* and *demonstrated* the good news of the Kingdom of God wherever He went, when He was here. He declared that this is why He was sent[2], and He engaged in the prophetic activities of the Father to demonstrate its power and presence upon the earth. This book will "bridge the gap" between Jesus' commission and humanity's original commission.

Genesis describes how this mandate is to be the supreme focus of humanity's attention, plans and activities upon the earth. It is to substantially motivate and impact our thoughts, attitudes and daily activities throughout our lifetime, from generation to generation, until completed. As a result, it is imperative that we effectively understand and align ourselves with its purpose, conditions, and desired results, as those who can actually make significant progress toward its completion.

We must recognize that this mandate God gave Adam and Eve in the Garden wasn't just for them. It didn't end or cease to be relevant to us when they committed high treason against God, rebelling against Him. Humanity wasn't disqualified nor were we released from it because "*we have all sinned and fall short of the glory of God*". As we will see, it is still in place and humanity is still being held accountable for its completion. It remains *mandatory* for every human being and every generation that has lived and will live upon the Earth. We must engage in an active, personal relationship with God and His prophetic Kingdom activities necessary to complete it.

---

2 Luke 4:43

9

There are many popular beliefs among the followers of Jesus, today, including; "the earth is not my home", "heaven is my home", and "I can't wait to leave the earth so I can get to heaven". It is these beliefs that determine our focus and motivate our activities during our lives here on the earth – "our reason for living". In Psalm 116:12-15, the Psalmist cries out to God, saying:

> *"What can I give back to the Lord for all the good things he has done for me? I'll lift up the cup of salvation. I'll call on the Lord's name. I'll keep the promises I made to the Lord in the presence of all God's people. The death of the Lord's faithful is a costly loss in his eyes."* Common English Bible

Why are the deaths of God's faithful servants a costly loss in His eyes? It is because these faithful, godly and spiritually mature members of the human community (God's servants) can actively participate and cooperate with Him in His earthly activities. When a vital, mature servant of God dies, it is one less human on the earth who is actively engaged in this endeavor.

In reality, the earth is our home; God gave it to humanity when He created us. It is the present evil system and culture operating upon the earth that is not our home. Heaven is not our home; it is a temporary residence for redeemed humanity until we receive our eternal, immortal bodies and return to the earth. Living in the presence of God and His Kingdom rule is our home. We were created to enjoy and experience His presence and Kingdom realities as we live upon and rule over the earth, as His regents. We will experience this reality, again!

Throughout the generations since achieving our victory over sin, through the death, burial and resurrection of Jesus, God has been steadily leading redeemed humanity into a greater understanding and experience of His Kingdom culture and realities. I believe, at this time in history and within the present spiritual experience of His Kingdom people, God is drawing our attention back to this Genesis mandate. Why? Because He knows, and as the scriptures describe, humanity cannot and will not move forward with the next phase of God's eternal purpose and plan for us until it is completed.

God hasn't forgotten the mandate and we must not ignore it. God has been inviting, leading, instructing and mentoring us over the centuries, to embrace these truths and realities that give us a greater understanding and experience of our victory over sin, through faith in Jesus. Embracing this greater understanding and personal experience has prepared us to, now, respond to God's invitations to move forward with Him. He is inviting us to embrace, better understand, pursue, and eventually complete our mandate. Seeing ourselves as God sees us and embracing His prophetic training for us is critical to engaging with Him in His Kingdom activities in our generation.

God is in the process of restoring humanity to a level of maturity and understanding that is capable of pursuing and completing this commission. God will not complete it for us. This is real and very practical; so practical, in fact, that Jesus demonstrated, instructed and coached His disciples in the practical application of these realities and activities. Jesus, being fully human, is our reliable example of how to respond to God, engage with Him in this regency role, and participate with Him in His prophetic Kingdom activities through the person and work of the Holy Spirit. The Holy Spirit is the most important Person and the most important relationship we have in this world, as followers of Jesus.

This mandate and its completion has been the context and driving force for God's plans, words and activities throughout human history, and brings clarity to all of the seemingly random events and activities that take place within our individual faith walks with Jesus. It gives them meaning, purpose and value; we can see that all of this is leading somewhere it and helps us appreciate all that God is doing in and through our lives. Even more, we will see what God expects of us and how we can recognize and respond to His invitations to join Him in His Kingdom activities, as we move forward toward the completion of our mandate, together.

Tom Casey (2020)

AUTHOR'S NOTE

Whether we realize it or not, we are all enrolled in a life-long training! God has been training humanity to know who He is and how to participate and cooperate with Him in His Kingdom realities and activities, since our creation. As followers of Jesus and covenant partners with God, through the new birth, we are enrolled in this training. Though this shouldn't be a surprise to us, it is to many of us. Throughout human history, God has given us example after example, generation after generation, of this training at work.

In more recent generations, humanity's overall "natural" knowledge has increased, dramatically. As we will see, the fact that knowledge has increased so dramatically is a biblical "sign" that we are living in the final days before Jesus returns. As "natural" knowledge has increased, so has our knowledge of God and the scriptures. Yet, as followers of Jesus, we have predominantly focused our attention on the intellectual and theological knowledge associated with our faith relationship with God. As a result, we are, generally, unlearned and, at times, resistant to the spiritual and experiential aspects of knowing God and the prophetic nature of His Kingdom activities. Even a cursory reading of the Bible reveals to us that God wants and intends for humanity to know and experience Him and the realities of His Kingdom, and not just know about them.

For nearly 50 years, I have been on a personal journey to know and experience the presence of God and His divine activities in my life. During these 50 years, I have experienced amazement, bewilderment, excitement, confusion, enlightenment, disappointment, and everything in between. I realized, early on, that this journey would be a training and that it would not be completed quickly or easily. Though the spiritual transition from darkness to light was immediate, the practical, experiential transition would take patience, persistence and faith throughout my lifetime. I knew this in theory, when I was young, but its reality became apparent as I grew older.

God's Kingdom training doesn't stop when this life is over. I am confident that we will continue to learn, experience and progress in the realities of God far into eternity. The more we learn and experience these realities, the more we realize there is so much more to learn and experience.

Several years ago, as I was completing my first book, *Studies In The Kingdom of God*, I realized I would be writing this book. That first book simply laid the foundation for what is being developed, here. As I complete this book, I am confident that other books will follow; each one building on what was established, previously.

This is how God has "wired" all of us. He created us to learn, experience, integrate, progress and mature. This is what His training is designed to accomplish, and this is how God mentors us, by the Holy Spirit, in who He is and how we can engage and cooperate with Him in the realities of His Kingdom. This training is preparing us for what is coming upon the world and for completing our divine mandate.

This book is a training manual. The content of each chapter builds upon the previous chapters. I include examples where appropriate and provide group questions at the end of each chapter. There is, also, a *Notes* section at the end of the book. This book is designed for group study, discussion and interaction, yet it can be used by individuals who are unable to participate in group learning activities. God trains us individually, but He also trains us together as a faith community. We learn better, together.

Stay engaged with the learning process God has established for your life. Don't try to rush through it because you can't. This is a life-long endeavor and we will only see the real benefits of His preparation, as we mature in it.

Tom Casey

CHAPTER 1

OUR MANDATE: GOD SHARES HIS EARTHLY RULE

"The heavens are Yours, the earth also is Yours; the world and all it contains, You have founded them." Psalm 89:11 NASB (emphasis mine)

*"The heavens belong to the Lord but **the earth He has given to all humanity**."* Psalm 115:16 NLT (emphasis mine)

Imagine this; the God and ruler of the entire universe actually places within His universe a race of beings created to specifically resemble and reflect His own glory and goodness. Not only that but the rest of His creation will freely recognize and rely upon them to lead and govern as if it was God doing it, Himself. These beings carry within themselves the very life, breath, nature and character qualities of God. They also possess the authority and ability to carry out God's will and activities, wherever and whenever He may desire.

Imagine that God created these beings for an eternal destiny and purpose that would far surpass anything they could possibly imagine. It would span His entire universe, challenge them in ways that only God, Himself, can devise and understand, and would bring such a growth and expansion of these beings that only the universe, itself, could contain and support their eternal activities.

Imagine that God lived and dwelt with these beings. They would enjoy each other's company, fellowship, interactions and activities as they got to know each other, more and more, throughout eternity. God would live with them on a single planet and would use this planet as a base of operations for their eternal ruling activities, together, throughout the universe. God would establish His throne on this planet and these individuals would live in a magnificent cube-like structure that extends 1,500 miles into the planet's atmosphere and outer space.

Imagine that God, for the purpose of individual and community growth, development, maturity and governance training, placed the initial two members of these image bearers, a man and a woman, upon this planet and gave them a mandate; to rule it, multiply upon it, fill it, and subdue it. These individuals would be God's resident representatives and regents to this planet and its inhabitants. Finally, after the successful completion of their mandate, God would launch these image bearers into the eternal plan and purpose He had destined for them.

Wow, what a story! Wouldn't this be a compelling premise for a grand novel? Yet, this is not a fictitious scenario. It is humanity's divinely established reality and destiny; God's eternal purpose and plan for all of humanity. It is playing out within our lives and before our very eyes, right now. Our willingness and effort to recognize, embrace, and passionately pursue this divine reality is the key to our fulfilling it.

God has predetermined and placed this divinely planned and orchestrated destiny squarely in front of all humanity, and He has equipped and provided us with everything we need to fully experience and accomplish it. We just need to know who God is, who we are, what He wants us to do, and how He wants us to do it. We're going to find out, together, what God has to say about this divine reality and what He has done to ensure that we reach our eternal destiny.

What Is The Kingdom of God?

To grasp the significance of humanity's eternal destiny and the mandate God has given us to complete, we must, first, know what the Kingdom of God is. In my previous book, *Studies In The Kingdom of God* [3], I spend considerable time explaining what the Kingdom of God is, how it operates, and how we can respond to and interact with it. In the book, I give a simple definition for the Kingdom of God:

---

[3] *"Studies In The Kingdom of God"* by Tom Casey, copyright 2017, Amazon Publishing

"A clear understanding of what the Scriptures tell us about the Kingdom of God is fundamentally important to our active involvement in the plan and activities of God. Therefore, I will give you a basic, scriptural definition of the Kingdom of God followed by what the Bible actually says about it. The Kingdom of God is the rule of God; the sovereignty and authority God possesses enabling Him to rule. As a result, the Kingdom of God is not limited to heaven, or the Church, or the earth.

Throughout the Scriptures, God's sovereignty and authority to rule is central to His purpose, plans and activities. Righteousness and justice must rule if peace and prosperity are to be the result. Mercy and truth must rule if love and life are to be the fruit. Only God is worthy of such dominion and capable of administrating such a government. It is an absolute blessing when God rules because the foundation of His sovereignty and authority (His throne) are righteousness, justice, mercy, and truth... they flow from His nature, as He rules. His government has ruled from eternity and it will continue to rule in the ages to come." [4]

The heavens declare the glory of God[5], and so must we! As high-ranking individuals within His Kingdom order, humanity is to extend God's universal rule to the earth and the creatures of the earth. We are to faithfully proclaim and demonstrate the nature, character, attributes and activities of God for all to see. We must know, understand and engage with God's *mode of operation;* what He does, why He does it, and how He carries out His ruling activities. As God's regents and representatives to the earth, we cannot separate our role and its responsibilities from the commission He gave us. We are told:

"With what shall I come before the Lord and bow down before the exalted God? Shall I come before him with burnt offerings, with calves a year old? Will the Lord be pleased with thousands of rams, with ten thousand rivers of olive

---

[4] Casey, Tom. *Studies In The Kingdom Of God: 2 Volumes In 1 Book* (Kindle Locations 602-611). Kindle Edition.

[5] Psalm 19:1-2

oil? Shall I offer my firstborn for my transgression, the fruit of my body for the sin of my soul? **He has shown you, O mortal, what is good. And what does the Lord require of you? To act justly and to love mercy and to walk humbly with your God."** [6]

We are to faithfully and humbly reflect God's nature and character and demonstrate His justice and mercy. The foundation of God's throne, the fundamental motives that fortify His sovereignty and authority to rule, is His nature and character. As His Kingdom representatives, who reflect His glory and cooperate with Him in His Kingdom activities, this must be our foundation, as well. Only then, will we successfully complete our mandate.

Understanding Who We Are And What We Are To Accomplish

The one true God, the Creator and Ruler of the entire universe, is the final authority on humanity, who we are, why He created us, and what we are to accomplish. All other opinions are just that, opinions, speculation and conjecture. If we want to find the answers to humanity's eternal purpose and destiny within this vast universe, we must go to God to find that out. At the same time, if we go to God to discover the truth, we must be willing to accept His response as the truth, and appropriately respond to it with assurance, faith and corresponding action. To do anything less, is to consider God and His word to be defective and unreliable.

In Psalm 82, God prophetically speaks through the psalmist, issuing an amazing declaration regarding humanity. In this declaration, God confirms an established reality involving humanity that is direct and unmistakable. At the same time, God acknowledges a subsequent reality, that we have brought upon ourselves, and must recognize. Through the psalmist, God declares:

*"**God takes his stand in the divine council; he gives judgment among the gods**; "How long will **you** judge unjustly by granting favor to the wicked? Selah Give justice to the lowly and the orphan; maintain the right of the poor and the destitute! Rescue the lowly and the needy.*

---

[6] Micah 6:6-8 NIV (emphasis mine)

Deliver them from the power of the wicked! **They don't know; they don't understand; they wander around in the dark. All the earth's foundations shake. I hereby declare, "You are gods, children of the Most High—all of you!.** *But you will die like mortals; you will fall down like any prince."* [7]

This is amazing! God, the Creator of all things, reflects on the realities and truths He has established within His universal rule. Then, with ultimate authority, He rises from His throne in Heaven to assert and declare humanity to be gods, His *image bearers*, within His Kingdom order.

Yes, God also acknowledges and identifies humanity's fallen condition and the effect it is having upon the earth.[8] He also acknowledges that, as a result of this fallen condition, humanity will physically die like mortals. Yet, humanity's fallen condition doesn't change the fact that God created humanity as His image bearers, eternal and immortal beings, and He confirms that fact. If it is true that God declares humanity to be in a fallen condition, because of sin, it is also true that God created humanity as His gods. He doesn't give us the option of picking and choosing what is truth and reality, and what isn't.

Jesus, Himself, confirms God's declaration to be true, by quoting this same scripture in Psalm 82, to the people He was talking and interacting with during His earthly ministry.[9] King David, who is described by God as *"a man after His own heart"*[10], realized and accepted this declared reality. David expresses it this way:

> *"When I look up at your skies, at what your fingers made— the moon and the stars that you set firmly in place—what are human beings that you think about them; what are human beings that you pay attention to them?* **You've made them only slightly less than divine, crowning them with glory and grandeur."** [11]

---

[7] Psalm 82:1-7 (CEB)

[8] Romans 8:18-25

[9] John 10:32-35 (CEB)

[10] 1Samuel 13:14

[11] Psalm 8:3-6 Common English Bible (CEB) (emphasis mine)

18

God created and positioned humanity to embody and reflect His glory, character qualities and righteous activities. We can't look at pagan mythology or modern-day comic books and movies as an accurate depiction of what it means to be a *god*. These depictions severely demean and vastly understate the true attributes of the One true God, and pervert the attributes and character qualities that humanity is to embody, reflect and demonstrate. As God's true image bearers, we can't allow these distorted depictions to keep us from recognizing and accepting ourselves for who we are created to be. We are created *"slightly less than divine"*, to reflect God's glory and majesty, and to cooperate with Him to conduct His ruling and governing activities on the earth, prophetically, as if He was here doing it, Himself:

> *"The Lord is the Spirit, and where the Lord's Spirit is, there is freedom.* ***All of us are looking with unveiled faces at the glory of the Lord as if we were looking in a mirror. We are being transformed into that same image from one degree of glory to the next degree of glory.*** *This comes from the Lord, who is the Spirit."* [12]

God said, *"You are gods, children of the Most High; all of you!"* We are His image bearers because of: 1) our intrinsic capacity and ability to resemble, reflect and represent the glory and image of the invisible God to all of His creation; and 2) our appointed and established position and role within His Kingdom order. At our creation, God declared:

> *"Let Us make man* ***in Our image, according to Our likeness***...*God created man* ***in His own image, in the image of God He created him; male and female*** *He created them.* ***God blessed them.****"* [13]

God sovereignly established it this way. What a divine purpose we have been given! What a unique status and privilege within the Kingdom of God we have been assigned in comparison to the rest of His creations! What a tremendous calling God has placed upon our lives within His dominion and hierarchy! *This is a profound truth*

---

[12] 2Corinthians 3:17-18 CEB (emphasis mine)
[13] Genesis 1:26-28a - NASB

and established reality that we must take seriously! We must see ourselves as God sees us if we are going to successfully reflect who He is and effectively cooperate with Him.

As a result, it's important for us to discover how we can embrace and implement this truth and reality so we remain *"doers of the word and not merely hearers, who delude themselves."*[14] Renewing our mind to think, see and speak the way God does is critical to changing our behavior and implementing these realities into our faith experience with Him. We must discover how to effectively reflect and demonstrate these godly attributes and activities. We cannot dismiss or ignore this reality if we want to fulfill our divine calling and purpose. This reality may be difficult for us to comprehend but that can't stop us from engaging with God to discover how we can "walk it out" in our faith experience with Him. God has a plan for us to embrace and implement this.

God's Representatives and Regents!

At humanity's creation, we were installed as God's *image bearers* and commissioned as His *regents* to the earth, to represent the Kingdom of God and to govern the earth and its inhabitants, as He would. What is a *regent* and what is its function? A *regent* is:

> *"A person who exercises the ruling power in a kingdom during the minority, absence, or disability of the sovereign."* Dictionary.com

> *"A substitute monarch, usually a trusted advisor or family member."* Vocabulary.com

Even though the word *regent* is not specifically used in the Bible, the role and function of a regent is described and personified many times in the scriptures. As God's commissioned representatives, we are authorized to rule, govern and subdue a specific domain, the Earth, with the authority God has given us. We are to engage in necessary communications and governing activities, involving the earth, on God's behalf. We received God's authority to rule and with it comes the necessary resources, tools and power to do so.

---

[14] James 1:22

One thing we must recognize and remember is that God is **always present** in all of His creation. He is never absent or unable to rule. So, when God placed us on the earth as His regents, it wasn't because He would be absent or in any way unable to rule. God commissioned humanity to rule the earth because He loves us as only God can. We are to rule the earth in the same manner God rules the universe, according to His godly character and attributes that He placed within us as His image bearers. As God rules from His throne with righteousness, justice and truth, humanity is to rule the earth with this same righteousness, justice and truth.

Humanity's Great Commission

As His image bearers and regents, God has declared our Kingdom destiny, role and initial assignment to all of His creation. In Genesis 1, in regard to His creation, specifically the earth, God assigned and commissioned humanity to a specific mandate:

> *"...let them rule over the fish of the sea and over the birds of the sky and over the cattle and over all the earth, and over every creeping thing that creeps on the earth"...."God said to them, "Be fruitful and multiply, and fill the earth, and subdue it; and rule over the fish of the sea and over the birds of the sky and over every living thing that moves on the earth.""* [15]

This was not a suggestion. It was not a request. It was a mandate; a unique, specific commission from God who, alone, rules the universe. God made it mandatory that we complete it. It will remain in force until all conditions identified within it are satisfied.

Genesis tells us that God *created humanity in His image*, He *created them male and female*, and He *blessed them*. When God created us, He blessed us; equipping and empowering us with everything we would need to accomplish this mandate. "Blessing" humanity was not a passive, feel good, "pat on the back". It was a proactive, complete empowering and equipping to act on His behalf, in all things pertaining to the earth. Humanity lacked NOTHING!

---

[15] Genesis 1:26-28 - NASB

We are to rule the earth in cooperation with God, not apart from Him. As God's regents, humanity is to carry out this commission and its associated activities, *in His name;* in His authority and with His provision, in any given situation. God's authority has been given to us and He makes His resources available to us, as the need arises. All we have to do is ask Him for them.[16]

To engage with Him in this way, it is important to know what He is saying, what He wants to do, and how He wants to conduct it. This is a *dynamic* responsibility and it requires a vital, *dynamic* relationship between God and His regents. Knowing God's will is critical to accomplishing His will. Knowing God personally is fundamental to knowing His will and how we are to cooperatively engage with Him in His desired activities.

With this in mind, let's review our commission in Genesis 1:26-28 and pay close attention to the specific terms and conditions it contains. This will help us identify what has already been completed and what remains to be completed:

- *Let them rule:*
  - *over all the earth*
  - *over the fish of the sea*
  - *over the birds of the sky*
  - *over the cattle*
  - *over every creeping thing that creeps on the earth*
  - *over every living thing that moves on the earth*
- *Be fruitful and multiply*
- *Fill the earth*
- *Subdue the entire earth*

These are the terms and conditions that must be met for completion. Humanity is to rule the entire earth and the creatures that inhabit it. Though we see a level of ruling that humanity has achieved, it is clear that we have more to accomplish. At the time of this writing, the earth has an approximate population of 7.8 billion and growing [17]. We are *filling* the earth, but we have not yet *filled* the earth.

---

[16] John 14:10-14; Matthew 7:7-11

[17] worldometers – 2020 (*www.worldometers.info*)

Looking at the final condition listed, we must ask, *"Why did God include the condition that humanity is to subdue the entire earth, if everything God created to inhabit the earth was pristine and already in perfect harmony with humanity? What on earth needed to be subdued?"* When this commission was declared, there was only one human on the earth: Adam. God made these declarations, not only for the benefit of Adam and the other humans who would follow him, but to inform the rest of His creation on the earth that humanity will rule it, on His behalf.

Our directive didn't end with humanity's rebellion in the Garden. God didn't rescind it when He banished Adam and Eve from it. God is still holding us accountable for its completion. God's people have a tremendous future ahead of us. We are so much more than we realize and will accomplish so much more than we can fathom. We are more than *sinners saved by grace.*

This is how He sees us and desires to relate to us. We are to reflect and demonstrate God's image and likeness, as well as His glory and grandeur within the regency relationship and role He has given us. *Our ability to regard ourselves as God regards us is crucial to our ability to work as co-laborers with Him.*

God is in the process of training and preparing humanity in how we are to successfully walk within our calling and cooperate with Him in His Kingdom activities. Acknowledging and pursuing this reality is necessary to accomplish all that God has planned for us, throughout eternity.

- *Takeaways for the reader:*

  o Recognizing and embracing what God thinks and says about us, as His gods, image bearers and regents is critical to our faith and ability to cooperate with Him in His Kingdom activities

  o The mandate God gave humanity at our creation is still in force and must be completed, if we are going to move forward with His eternal plans for us.

- *Small group questions*:

  - o We must recognize that humanity are still gods, image bearers and regents in God's eyes, even though we sinned against Him in the Garden. How should that impact our relationship with God and our every-day life of faith with Him, moving forward?
  - o Do you think that completing God's mandate for humanity is still a realistic goal? What can we do, now, to be a participant in its completion? What are our major roadblocks?

CHAPTER 2

DELAYED BUT NOT DISQUALIFIED

*"The snake was the most intelligent of all the wild animals that the LORD God had made. He said to the woman, "**Did God really say** that you shouldn't eat from any tree in the garden?"* Genesis 3:1 Common English Bible (CEB) (emphasis mine)

*"The snake said to the woman, "**You won't die!** God knows that on the day you eat from it, you will see clearly and **you will be like God**, knowing good and evil."* Genesis 3:4-5 CEB (emphasis mine)

God's mandate for humanity includes several conditions that must be satisfied in order to be fulfilled. One of these conditions is to *"...fill the earth, **and subdue it**."* Wasn't the earth and the creatures God placed upon it pristine and perfect? What was on the earth that needed to be subdued?

Even though the native creatures of the earth were living in harmony with humanity and God, there was a *presence* upon the earth that was not in harmony, at least not with God. This creature was *on* the earth, but it was not *of* the earth; it was not created to dwell upon the earth. It was from another domain within God's Kingdom. It had been banished from heaven to the earth because of its treasonous and subversive activities against God. Likewise, it had no intention of peacefully submitting to humanity's authority over the earth, either.

This being was highly intelligent and, at one time, was *"full of wisdom and beauty, the image of perfection"*.[18] While in heaven, it had been *"covered with gold and every precious stone"*. It was created to be a guardian. It was the anointed angel on God's holy mountain; stationed at the throne of God where it *"walked among the stones of fire"*.[19] This angel we know as Lucifer, also called

---

[18]Ezekiel 28:12 Common English Bible (CEB)

Satan, wasn't satisfied with God's appointed position for him. He wanted more; he wanted to rule. Dwelling and serving at the throne of God wasn't enough for him. He wanted to sit on the throne. Being the guardian of the throne of God wasn't enough. Lucifer wanted to make himself *"like the Most High"*. [20]

Having been banished by God to the earth because of his blatant treason and rebellion, Satan became enraged when he saw God's creation of humanity. He seethed with anger as he saw God create humanity *"slightly less than divine";* gods, who had the ability to resemble and reflect God's image and glory. He raged when God commissioned humanity to rule the earth as His chosen regents and gave them His authority and divine provision to carry it out. What Satan coveted, God embodied in and gave to humanity. Satan was so enraged and jealous that he set himself to ruin and destroy humanity before they were able to complete their mandate.

As a spiritual being, Satan inhabited the physical body of a snake, in the Garden. He wanted to approach humanity (Adam and Eve) deceptively, coming to them by stealth as one of the earthly creatures they were familiar with and ruled over. Satan knew, as a present inhabitant of the earth, he was subject to humanity's authority. Instead of engaging in overt rebellion against Adam and Eve, as he did against God, he did so through subversive means – *deceptive misinformation.*

By asking Eve the simple question, *"Did God really say...?"*, Satan sought to determine: 1) how mature humanity was in their relationship with God, and 2) would they exercise their authority to subdue the earth, including him, if they were challenged? Eve and Adam listened to Satan's words instead of using their God-given authority to cast him out of the Garden. They were, both, mesmerized and lured at the prospect of becoming more like God than they already were. They hadn't, yet, grasped the reality that they were already gods within the Kingdom of God, being able to resemble, reflect and demonstrate the image, glory and activities of God.

---

[19] Ezekiel 28:12-19
[20] Isaiah 14:13-14

Satan discovered that they were immature in their position and relationship with God. He discovered that they weren't willing to exercise their God-given authority to subdue him, removing him from the earth. Instead, being mesmerized and enticed, they "took the bait" and ate of the forbidden tree. As a result, humanity relinquished their earthly authority, giving it to Satan and submitting to him as their earthly lord and ruler.

God's response to all of this is recorded for us in Genesis 3:

> *"So the LORD God said to the serpent, "Because you have done this, "Cursed are you above all livestock and all wild animals! You will crawl on your belly and you will eat dust all the days of your life. And I will put enmity* (contempt) *between you and the woman, and between your offspring and hers; he will crush your head, and you will strike his heel." To the woman he said, "I will make your pains in childbearing very severe; with painful labor you will give birth to children. Your desire will be for your husband, and he will rule over you." To Adam he said, "Because you listened to your wife and ate fruit from the tree about which I commanded you, 'You must not eat from it,' "Cursed is the ground because of you; through painful toil you will eat food from it all the days of your life. It will produce thorns and thistles for you, and you will eat the plants of the field. By the sweat of your brow you will eat your food until you return to the ground, since from it you were taken; for dust you are and to dust you will return."[21]*

God's judgment was dire and devastating. Yet, we can hold on to one important fact: Even though humanity surrendered their authority to rule the earth, God did not disqualify them. Humanity's mandate to rule as God's regents on the earth was delayed but it wasn't canceled.

Yet, what good is retaining the role of a regent if we have no authority to enforce that rule? It's even worse than that. What good is the role of a regent when the authority you possess is willingly surrendered to another, who despises you, uses that authority to enslave you, abuses you, desires to make your entire natural life

---

[21]Genesis 3:14-19 NASB

absolutely miserable, and relishes the thought of you spending eternity with him experiencing God's judgment? Humanity suddenly found themselves on the precipice of God's eternal judgment with, seemingly, no hope in sight.

Nevertheless, when God pronounced His judgment, specifically the curses upon the serpent and Satan, He cryptically and prophetically declared that Satan's authority to rule the earth and subject humanity to his tyrannical rule would not last forever. God declared:

> *"So the LORD God said to the serpent, "Because you have done this, "Cursed are you above all livestock and all wild animals! You will crawl on your belly and you will eat dust all the days of your life. And **I will put enmity** (contempt) **between you and the woman, and between your offspring and hers; he will crush your head, and you will strike his heel."""* [22]

As a curse upon him, God prophetically declared to Satan that an offspring of the woman will *"crush your head"*, at the same time that *"you will strike his heel"*. A member of the human family will come and inflict an eternal "death blow" to Satan's authority over humanity and the earth (crush Satan's head). At the same time, Satan will inflict a "bruise" upon this person's heel (a minor, temporary imposition). The authority that humanity surrendered, through deceptive means, will be restored so we can, once again, stand in our place within the Kingdom of God.

God, in His mercy and grace, will restore to humanity all that we had lost, through the eventual eternal defeat of Satan. God took the first prophetic step in restoring humanity. God has given humanity a firm and undeniable hope that what we began at our creation, we will complete. In the next chapter, we will discover the first major milestone in God's plan and process for working with humanity to complete our great commission.

- *Takeaways for the reader*:

---

[22] Genesis 3:14-15 NASB (emphasis mine)

- Even though humanity sinned and committed treason against God, we have not been disqualified from our position as image bearers of God within His Kingdom, and God has not rescinded our position as His regents upon the earth
- God told us that a member of the human family will come to reinstate humanity to our rightful place in God's created order, restoring our authority so we can successfully complete our divine mandate

- *Small group questions*:

  - What does the account of humanity's rebellion against God in the Garden tell us about the role and ability of deception and misinformation in Satan's arsenal of weapons?
  - What can we do to prepare ourselves for and resist these deceptive weapons, when they are used against us?

CHAPTER 3

GOD'S ETERNAL DEVOTION TO HUMANITY: THE BLOOD COVENANT

*"So the L*ORD *said to him, "Bring me a heifer, a goat and a ram, each three years old, along with a dove and a young pigeon."* **Abram brought all these to him, cut them in two and arranged the halves opposite each other...When the sun had set and darkness had fallen, a smoking firepot with a blazing torch appeared and passed between the pieces. On that day the L**ORD **made a covenant with Abram..."** Genesis 15:9-10, 17-18 NASB (emphasis mine)

"When Abram was 99 years old, the Lord appeared to Abram and said to him, "I am El Shaddai. **Walk with me and be trustworthy. I will make a covenant between us** *and I will give you many, many descendants." Abram fell on his face, and* **God said to him, "But me, my covenant is with you;** *you will be the ancestor of many nations."* **"I will set up my covenant with you and your descendants after you in every generation as an enduring covenant. I will be your God and your descendants' God after you." "This is my covenant that you and your descendants must keep: Circumcise every male.** *You must circumcise the flesh of your foreskins, and* **it will be a symbol of the covenant between us.**" Genesis 17:1-11 CEB (emphasis mine)

"And in the same way He took the cup after they had eaten, saying, **"This cup which is poured out for you is the new covenant in My blood."** Luke 22:20 NASB (emphasis mine)

God is completely committed to humanity, whether it is to the successful completion of our mandate or to the realization of our eternal destiny! He communicates and demonstrates this commitment to us, continually!

Following humanity's fall, we can see the results of sin's destructive effects upon the human race and the earth. We can see a steady decline in our ability to effectively understand God's place in our lives, as well as our place within His Kingdom order. With few exceptions, God was being pushed out of the human experience. This wasn't God's fault. The hearts and minds of people were being enslaved and corrupted because of sin. At the same time, Satan and his evil forces continued to establish their authoritative dominance over the earth. The "domain of darkness" was tightening its grip on humanity and this world's system of operation.

Yet, in the midst of all of this, God had a plan that would restore humanity to Him, as a "community of faith'. Included in this restoration would be the authority to reestablish ourselves as God's image bearers and regents. God can assist us by doing what we are incapable of doing for ourselves. For humanity to be successful, God must: 1) rescue and free humanity from the shackles of sin and the domain of darkness, and 2) reveal, instruct, train and mentor humanity in who He is and who we are, within His created Kingdom order. This will not be an easy task for us, nor a quick work for God because it will require working with humanity over many, many generations, and over a long period of time, to accomplish.

The Human Dilemma

To put this monumental effort into perspective, let's look at a few facts. The effects of sin over the millennia has dulled humanity's ability to recognize, respond to, and interact with God in a meaningful way. Humanity has become, almost exclusively, "naturally-minded". God is spirit[23] and He lives in Heaven. He is not like anyone or anything we have encountered upon the earth. As the human community, we claim to know a lot about God and understand how He operates. Yet, in reality, to say that we know and understand God is like saying a new-born baby knows and understands quantum physics. We consider our natural selves and earthly activities, and dare to equate them with God; who He is and how He conducts His Kingdom activities. Nothing could be further from the truth, and reality.

---

[23] John 4:24

God has spoken to and interacted with humanity countless times throughout our history. Yet, we have only "scratched the surface" of knowing and understanding Him in any real way. God brings our arrogant presumptions to our attention in Psalm 50, when He says:

> *"Why do you talk about my laws? Why do you even mention my covenant (faithful decree)? You hate discipline, and you toss my words behind your back. You make friends with thieves whenever you see one; you spend your time with adulterers. You set your mouth free to do evil, then harness your tongue to tell lies. You sit around, talking about your own siblings; you find fault with the children of your very own mother. **You've done these things and I've kept quiet. You thought I was just like you!** But now I'm punishing you; I'm laying it all out, right in front of your face. So consider this carefully..."* [24]

This is a very revealing statement that tells us a lot about who God is and why we make little progress in our ability to know and understand Him. We think God is mostly disinterested with humanity and what goes on here because He doesn't seem to immediately and explicitly respond to our acts of wickedness and injustice. We consider this "silence" to be indifference or that all of this is "beneath Him". We tell ourselves that God must have more important things to do, or He has lost interest in us and doesn't really care what we do. As a result, humanity has no fear or apprehension of equating ourselves with God. We quote the Bible and "speak for God" when it serves our purposes, as if we confidently understand what He would do or say in a given situation. We have no fear of discipline or retribution for considering ourselves to be on the same level of existence and understanding with God.

This is how far humanity has fallen since our creation. This is the reality of where we are, in our relationship to God. At the same time, this must be the starting point for God if He is going to implement a plan to reveal, instruct, train and mentor us in who He is and the realities of His Kingdom. To prove that He is not like us, God didn't "blink an eye" when He established His plan to do just this. God doesn't worry and fret when He thinks about the effort

---

[24] Psalm 50:16-23 Common English Bible (CEB) (emphasis mine)

and time it will take to see this plan reach its completion. He loves humanity and is willing to sacrifice everything to see us restored to Him and our original place within His Kingdom order.

To initiate this restoration process and plan, God is going to extend a personal invitation to a specific person that, if accepted, will set in motion the divine revealing, instructing, training and mentoring activities required to restore humanity and eventually bring our great commission to its completion.

Abraham, The Friend of God

Around 2000 B.C., approximately 400 years after The Flood and 200 years after the rebellion at the Tower of Babel, there lived a man named Abram in a place called Haran. In Genesis 12, God engages with and speaks to Abram:

> *"The Lord said to Abram, "Leave your land, your family, and your father's household for the land that I will show you. I will make of you a great nation and will bless you. I will make your name respected, and you will be a blessing. I will bless those who bless you, those who curse you I will curse; all the families of the earth will be blessed because of you." "Abram left just as the Lord told him."* [25]

Abram was 75 years old when he accepted God's invitation to follow Him. Of all the people living on the earth at that time, there was something in the heart and life of Abram that was open to God engaging with him and relating to him in a meaningful way. Abram responded to God by leaving Haran with his wife, Sarai, and his nephew, Lot. Throughout their journey, God blessed Abram tremendously and protected and provided for him and those who were with him. Arriving in Bethel, Abram asked his nephew Lot to separate himself, his family, and his possessions from Abram. They each had been blessed by God with so many possessions and livestock that they were over-running the land, and it was causing strife between their households.

---

[25] Genesis 12:1-4 CEB

Once Lot and his family and possessions were separated from Abram, we see a whole new level of relationship and interaction between God and Abram occur. In Genesis 13, we are told:

> *"The Lord said to Abram, after Lot had separated from him, "Now lift up your eyes and look from the place where you are, northward and southward and eastward and westward; for all the land which you see, I will give it to you and to your descendants forever. I will make your descendants as the dust of the earth, so that if anyone can number the dust of the earth, then your descendants can also be numbered. Arise, walk about the land through its length and breadth; for I will give it to you."* [26]

God invited Abram to embark on a unique and personal relationship and journey with Him. This promise set in motion the divine relationship, realities and activities required to eventually restore humanity. As the relationship between God and Abram became stronger, their faithfulness toward one another also became stronger; they became friends. One day, God appeared to Abram:

> *"...the word of the Lord came to Abram in a vision, saying, "Do not fear, Abram, I am a shield to you; Your reward shall be very great." Abram said, "O Lord God, what will You give me, since I am childless, and the heir of my house is Eliezer of Damascus?" And Abram said, "Since You have given no offspring to me, one born in my house is my heir."* [27]

Until this moment, throughout the initial years of their relationship, God made promises to Abram and gave him prophetic insight into what He would do in and through him and his descendants. Yet, until this specific interaction, Abram had not responded to God with the question that was troubling him the most about all of these promises:

> *"O Lord God, **what will You give me, since I am childless, and the heir of my house is Eliezer of Damascus?"** And Abram said, **"Since You have given***

---

[26] Genesis 13:14-17 NASB
[27] Genesis 15:1-3 NASB

no offspring to me, one born in my house is my heir."

We know this issue of having no son had been troubling Abram for some time because as soon as God began to speak to him in the vision, Abram spoke up and asked Him about an heir from his own body. Abram couldn't believe God for the completion of these wonderful promises because he couldn't see how it would ever happen, not having a son. Not only that, but being over 75 years old, he couldn't see how having a son was even an option. Abram was in serious doubt about these promises from God, and it was becoming more and more difficult to believe God for them.

Then, hearing from Abram's own mouth, the doubts he had concerning God's promises to him, God responded:

> *"Then behold,* **the word of the Lord came to him, saying,** *"This man will not be your heir; but* **one who will come forth from your own body, he shall be your heir.***" And He took him outside and said, "Now look toward the heavens, and count the stars, if you are able to count them." And He said to him, "So shall your descendants be."* **Then he believed in the Lord; and He reckoned it to him as righteousness.***" [28]*

This burning question from Abram and God's response and declaration to him changed everything for Abram. It is also an important lesson for us to learn. It is the foundation for the active, vital and trusting relationship God established with Abram, and that He wants to have with each of us. Not only does God desire a unique, personal and daily interactive relationship with us, He wants us to be honest and truthful with Him about our relationship.

God has a unique, personal calling and purpose for each of our lives, with promises attached to it. He designed His plan for us and our interactions with Him to be "beyond ourselves". We are God's image bearers and regents, and we are supposed to interact with Him prophetically and supernaturally. The Bible tells us that to see the promises of God come to pass, we must believe Him for things that are outside of our control; beyond our ability to conduct and

---

[28] Genesis 15:4-6 NASB (emphasis mine)

accomplish, without Him. We will need to engage in activities with Him that only He can accomplish. God designed it this way.

This is a prophetic, supernatural relationship we have committed ourselves to, with God! We should expect it and not approach Him and it in any other way! At the same time, we must be honest with God about our thoughts and feelings throughout our relationship. He cares and wants us to communicate these things to Him. Not that He doesn't already know what we think and feel, but He wants us to communicate them as a means of acknowledging them, honestly, to ourselves. Only when we are honest with Him and ourselves, can He effectively work to help us confront and overcome those things that would hinder our faith in Him and His promises for us.

In our relationship with Him, God doesn't "go through the motions". Nor, does He want us to go through the motions of making it appear that we are in a relationship with Him, when we really aren't. If we do, we are only fooling ourselves; we aren't fooling Him. When it comes to completing our mandate, we have tremendous promises that God has given to us. Yet, unless we approach our relationship with Him in an honest, meaningful and transparent way, that relationship will not grow and mature, and we will come up short of all that God intends for us.

The Covenant

After Abram opened his heart to God about what was troubling him and keeping him from believing His promises, God then promised Abram a son, through whom the promises would be fulfilled. Now, with his questions answered and his concerns alleviated, Abram was able to respond to God's promises in true faith. As a result of his faith being actively exercised, God was able to "reckon" Abram's faith as righteousness. The word "reckon" in this verse, means to *"esteem, calculate, invent, make a judgment, imagine, count."* [29] God saw Abram's faith being actively exercised in Him and His promises. As a result, God esteemed and counted Abram's faith as righteousness.

---

[29] The NASB Old Testament Hebrew Lexicon (online)

This event was a major milestone in the relationship between God and Abram. They had already achieved a healthy level of honesty, trust and faithfulness within their relationship. Now, as a result of this interaction between them, God, according to His plan, was ready to initiate and establish the first major milestone in His efforts to restore humanity to their rightful position and authority within His Kingdom. God instructed Abram, saying:

> *"Bring Me a three-year-old heifer, and a three year old female goat, and a three year old ram, and a turtledove, and a young pigeon." Then he brought all these to Him and cut them in two, and laid each half opposite the other; but he did not cut the birds."* [30]

When God spoke to Abram and he heard His instructions, Abram did not hesitate. He quickly responded because he recognized and knew what God was about to do. God's next actions were going to profoundly impact their relationship, moving forward. The scriptures tell us:

> *"Then he brought all these to Him and cut them in two, and laid each half opposite the other; but he did not cut the birds. **The birds of prey came down upon the carcasses, and Abram drove them away.**"* [31]

After placing the animal pieces on the ground, Abram took aggressive action against the birds of prey, to keep them from disturbing the animal pieces. Why? Because what he and God were about to engage in was considered, within his culture, a very solemn and meaningful ceremony; one not to be approached or entered into quickly or flippantly. As Abram and God were about to engage in this solemn ceremony, he was surprised by what happened next and the unique "twist" this ceremony was taking. The scriptures tell us:

> *"Now when the sun was going down, **a deep sleep fell upon Abram; and behold, terror and great darkness fell upon him.**"* [32]

---

[30] Genesis 15:9-10 NASB
[31] Genesis 15:10-11 NASB (emphasis mine)
[32] Genesis 15:12 NASB (emphasis mine)

Abram was anxiously preparing himself to engage with God in this friendship ritual. What surprised Abram is that he suddenly fell into a deep sleep and an ominous fear and darkness surrounded him. Abram discovered that all he could do is lay there on the ground, as a spectator, and witness what was about to happen. As he lay on the ground, the scriptures tell us:

> "God said to Abram, "**Know for certain** that your descendants will be strangers in a land that is not theirs, where they will be enslaved and oppressed four hundred years. But I will also judge the nation whom they will serve, and afterward they will come out with many possessions. As for you, **you shall go to your fathers in peace; you will be buried at a good old age. Then in the fourth generation they will return here,** for the iniquity of the Amorite is not yet complete." It came about when the sun had set, that it was very dark, and behold, **there appeared a smoking oven and a flaming torch which passed between these pieces. On that day the Lord made a covenant with Abram,** saying, "**To your descendants I have given this land,** from the river of Egypt as far as the great river, the river Euphrates." [33]

What Abram recognized from God's instructions is that God was preparing for what is known as a *blood covenant*. A blood covenant is an ancient ceremony, as old as humanity itself, where two or more parties enter into a mutual, solemn and binding relationship and agreement with each other, for a specific purpose. This relationship is much more than a contract and is considered to be much stronger than the legal agreements we arrange and enter into today. Our contracts and legal relationships today often contain "back door clauses" and "escape clauses" that allow us a way out of the agreement and relationship, if we find it doesn't suit us. A blood covenant is very different and, as such, it should not be entered into without a clear understanding of what the relationship and agreement will entail, and after serious consideration of its terms, conditions and penalties.

Blood Covenants are central to the Bible, to our understanding of

---

[33] Genesis 15:13-18 NASB (emphasis mine)

the nature of God, and to the relationship, agreement and commitments we have with Him as His Kingdom people. Understanding the blood covenant and how God has used it to establish His relationships, purposes and plans with humanity will change the way we approach and view God. It will also affect the way we view ourselves, our relationship with God, His promises to us, and the Kingdom resources and activities He has made available to us.

In his book, *The Blood Covenant*,[34] H. Clay Trumbull gives us wonderful examples and some specific details of what a blood covenant is, the types of blood covenants humanity has developed, what its impact has been upon humanity over the millennia, and why the blood covenant has been used by humanity to establish their most binding relationships and agreements. God understands the importance and solemn nature of the blood covenant relationship within the human community, and He chose to enact it in His relationship with Abram and humanity. In regard to the blood covenant, Trumbull tells us:

> As an ancient Semitic ritual, *"the rite of blood-covenanting is a form of covenanting by which two persons enter into the closest, the most enduring, and the most sacred of compacts, as friends and brothers, or as more than brothers, through the inter-commingling of their blood, by means of its mutual tasting, or of its inter-transfusion."* [35]

Trumbull continues his explanation of the blood covenant by describing an instance of two young Syrian men who had been friends for years, and had decided to become *"brother-friends, in the covenant of blood"*. Trumbull describes what took place during this blood-covenanting ceremony:

> *"It was two young men, who were to enter into this covenant...Their relatives and neighbors were called together, in the open place before the village fountain, to witness the sealing compact. The young men publicly announced their purpose, and their reasons for it. Their*

[34] *The Blood Covenant* by H. Clay Trumbull Copyright 1975, 2009 by Impact Books, Inc. (now Impact Christian Books)

[35] *Ibid.*, pages 4-5

declarations were written down in duplicate – one paper for each friend – and signed by themselves and by several witnesses.

One of the friends took a sharp lancet and opened a vein in the other's arm. Into the opening thus made, he inserted a quill, through which he sucked the living blood. The lancet-blade was carefully wiped on one of the duplicate covenant-papers, and then it was taken by the other friend, who made a like incision in its first-users arm, and drank his blood through the quill, wiping the blade on the duplicate covenant-record. The two friends declared together: "We are brothers in a covenant made before God: who deceiveth the other, him will God deceive." Each blood-marked covenant-record was then folded carefully, to be sewed up in a small leather case, or amulet, about an inch square; to be worn thenceforward by one of the covenant-brothers, suspended about his neck, or bound upon the arm, in token of the indissoluble relation." [36]

Trumbull continues, by saying:

There are many forms of Semitic covenanting, *"but this is the extremest and most sacred of them all. As it is the inter-commingling of very lives, nothing can transcend it. It forms a tie, or a union, which cannot be dissolved. In marriage, divorce is a possibility: not so in the covenant of blood. Although now comparatively rare, in view of its responsibilities and of its indissolubleness, this covenant is sometimes entered into by confidential partners in business, or by fellow-travelers."*

"Yet again, it is the chosen compact of loving friends; of those who are drawn to it only by mutual love and trust. He who has entered into this compact with another, counts himself the possessor of a double life; for his friend, whose blood he has shared, is ready to lay down his life with him, or for him. Hence the leather case...containing the record of the covenant, is counted a proud badge of honor by one who possesses it; and he has an added sense of security, because

---

[36] Ibid,; pages 5-6

he will not be alone when he falleth." [37]

There are many types of blood covenants that have been developed and enacted throughout the earth, from time immemorial. Yet, in every case, it is considered to be the most sacred, personal and enduring relationship and agreement a person can enter into with another person. Blessings and curses are a part of these blood covenants. Gifts and tokens of commitment and faithfulness are a part of them. In some cases, everything that belongs to the one covenant partner is now made available to the other partner. In some extreme rituals, if one of the blood-covenant partners breaks the covenant, the other partner and his family can hunt him down and kill him, for breaking it. The blood covenant is not for the faint of heart.

Abram was well-aware of the blood covenant and its meaning. This is why God chose to "cut the covenant" with him, after their relationship had been in place for a number of years. They had become close, faithful friends. Was it necessary for God to hold Himself accountable for His promises made to Abram, with this blood covenant? No. God is forever faithful and for Him to lie or not follow through with a promise or declaration is to deny Himself and who He is. When God makes a promise, even a conditional promise, and that condition is met, God will see to it that the promise is fulfilled.

No, God did not enter into this blood covenant for Himself. He entered into it for Abram. God knew that Abram needed proof that the promises He had made to him would be fulfilled. It is the weakness of humanity and our lack of relationship and faith in God that necessitated this blood covenant. Abram knew that if God failed to deliver on His promises, as a result of this covenant, His name and reputation could no longer be trusted; they would be worthless. Abram knew he would have a son, an heir from his own body. His descendants would be as numerous as the sand on the seashore and as the stars in the sky. The entire earth would be blessed through him. As a result of this covenant, Abram knew that all of these promises from God would be fulfilled. This blood covenant is for Abram and his descendants; it is for us!

---

[37] *Ibid.*, pages 6-8

What is amazing about this particular blood covenant between God and Abram is that God did not require Abram to participate in it, on an equal footing with Him. God did not require anything from Abram. This was a blood covenant enacted by God, alone, and Abram and his descendants are the sole beneficiaries of the terms, promises and benefits associated with it. The responsibility for executing and successfully delivering all terms, promises and benefits of the entire covenant belonged to God. God placed Abram (and his descendants) in the position of being receivers and beneficiaries, only. God put His name and His reputation, as well as His Kingdom possessions and resources on the line, expecting nothing in return; at least not at this time.

Once again, here are the terms, conditions, promises, responsibilities and outcomes of the covenant God enacted with Abram and his descendants that day:

- Know for certain:

  o your descendants will be strangers in a land that is not theirs, where they will be enslaved and oppressed four hundred years

  o I will judge the nation whom they will serve

  o afterward they will come out with many possessions

  o you shall go to your fathers in peace; you will be buried at a good old age

  o in the fourth generation they will return to this land

To seal the covenant, God "walked" between the divided animal parts and the blood that had been spilled, *swearing by Himself* that He would keep the promises made to Abram and His descendants, forever. Not only was God sealing the promises He made at that ceremony, *He was also sealing all of the previous promises He had made to Abram and His descendants.*

There were no responsibilities placed on Abram. All of it was on God to fulfill:

"It came about when the sun had set, that it was very dark,

*and behold, **there appeared a smoking oven and a flaming torch which passed between these pieces. On that day the Lord made a covenant with Abram,** saying, "To your descendants I have given this land, from the river of Egypt as far as the great river, the river Euphrates."* [38]

When God appeared and entered into the covenant with Abram, He appeared in the representative images of a *smoking oven* and a *flaming torch*. By appearing to Abram (and us) in this way, God is communicating to us two important characteristics about Himself; who He is (a righteous God, a consuming fire[39]), and that He will relate to and interact with humanity (a lamp to our feet and a light to our path[40]) in this way, moving forward. With this blood covenant, God established the first milestone in His plan to restore humanity to their rightful place and function within His Kingdom order. God is for us and has committed Himself and the resources of His entire Kingdom to restore us and provide us with everything we need to complete our mandate:

> *"Now lift up your eyes and look from the place where you are, northward and southward and eastward and westward; for all the land which you see, **I will give it to you and to your descendants forever. I will make your descendants as the dust of the earth**, so that if anyone can number the dust of the earth, then your descendants can also be numbered."* [41]

How do we know that God's covenant and promises with Abram are for all of us – for all of humanity, and not only for the natural descendants of Abram, the Jewish people? God tells us through the Apostle Paul, in the book of Romans:

> *"**The promise to Abraham and to his descendants, that he would inherit the world, didn't come through the Law but through the righteousness that comes from faith.** If they inherit because of the Law,*

---

[38] Genesis 15:8-18 NASB

[39] Hebrews 12:28-29

[40] Psalm 119:105

[41] Genesis 13:14-16 NASB (emphasis mine)

then faith has no effect and the promise has been canceled. The Law brings about wrath. But when there isn't any law, there isn't any violation of the law. **That's why the inheritance comes through faith, so that it will be on the basis of God's grace. In that way, the promise is secure for all of Abraham's descendants, not just for those who are related by Law but also for those who are related by the faith of Abraham, who is the father of all of us.** *As it is written: "I have appointed you to be the father of many nations".* **So Abraham is our father in the eyes of God in whom he had faith,** *the God who gives life to the dead and calls things that don't exist into existence."* [42]

God's enduring covenant with Abraham is for all of humanity, who possess and exercise the same faith in God as Abraham did, and it binds God to us, forever. As a result of God's blood covenant with Abraham, we are covenant partners with God through our exercise of this same kind of faith. *God, Himself, and what belongs to Him are at our disposal, as His covenant partners of faith. He enacted this so we can all know Him, grow in Him, respond to Him, engage with Him, and cooperate with Him in His Kingdom realities and activities, forever! This is the commitment God has made to humanity, who exercise the same faith in Him as Abraham did!*

This is why we must understand the significance of and power behind the blood covenant. It communicates to us God's complete commitment and devotion to humanity, as well as the fact that He and His entire Kingdom's resources and power are focused on our success. This blood covenant should settle in our hearts and minds, once and for all, that we can trust in and rely on God to be for us and to act on our behalf, moving forward, in every generation.

The Mark of the Covenant

Later in their relationship, after it has matured even more, God does ask Abraham and his descendants, as a faith community, to commit themselves to Him, as their God. As a sign of their commitment to Him, God instructs Abraham and his descendants to "cut the

---

[42] Romans 4:13-17 CEB (emphasis mine)

44

covenant" with Him":

> *"Now when Abram was ninety-nine years old, the Lord appeared to Abram and said to him, "**I am God Almighty; walk before Me, and be blameless. I will establish My covenant between Me and you,** and I will multiply you exceedingly." Abram fell on his face, and God talked with him, saying, "**As for Me,** behold, **My covenant is with you, And you will be the father of a multitude of nations. No longer shall your name be called Abram, but your name shall be Abraham; For I have made you the father of a multitude of nations.** I will make you exceedingly fruitful, and **I will make nations of you, and kings will come forth from you.***
>
> ***I will establish My covenant between Me and you and your descendants after you throughout their generations for an everlasting covenant, to be God to you and to your descendants after you.*** *I will give to you and to your descendants after you, the land of your sojournings, all the land of Canaan, for an everlasting possession; **and I will be their God.**" God said further to Abraham, "Now as for you, you shall keep My covenant, you and your descendants after you throughout their generations. **This is My covenant, which you shall keep,** between Me and you and your descendants after you: **every male among you shall be circumcised. And you shall be circumcised in the flesh of your foreskin, and it shall be the sign of the covenant between Me and you.***" [43]

As we look at this aspect of the blood covenant, there are several noticeable differences from the previous version:

- God stipulates that Abraham and his descendants should conduct themselves blamelessly in their relationship with Him

- God declares that a multitude of kings and nations will be of Abraham's descendants

---

[43] Genesis 17:1-11 NASB (emphasis mine)

- God changes Abram's name to Abraham, to reflect and communicate the realities of God's covenant promises
- God also stipulates that Abraham and his descendants will recognize and follow Him, *El Shaddai*, *"the God who is more than enough"* as their God, forever
- Abraham and his male descendants will be physically circumcised as the mark or sign of their blood covenant with God

As a result of the relationship God and Abraham have developed over the years, God now places some demands and responsibilities upon Abraham and his descendants, as their obligations to the covenant. This is not a new blood covenant between them; it is an extension of the original covenant. This is another major milestone in God's plan to restore humanity. Abraham has proven to God to be a faithful friend. As such, God wants Abraham to bear some responsibility toward Him in their relationship, moving forward. God saw something in Abraham that motivated Him to choose him and to pursue Abraham as a friend and blood covenant partner. God tells us what that quality is, in Genesis 18:

> *"For I have chosen him,* **so that he may command his children and his household after him to keep the way of the Lord by doing righteousness and justice,** *so that the Lord may bring upon Abraham what He has spoken about him."* [44]

God chose Abraham *"because he would be faithful to act with justice and righteousness, and he would faithfully raise his children to do the same"*. God knew His plan to restore humanity would take generation upon generation to complete. So, He chose a friend and covenant partner who would instruct his children and his children's children to be faithful to Him, throughout their generations.

God has now expressed His love, devotion and commitment to humanity by expressing it to His friend and covenant partner, Abraham, and his descendants. In return, Abraham and his descendants express their love, devotion, faith and commitment to

---

[44] Genesis 18:19 NASB

God as their friend and covenant partner, forever. Abraham and his descendants will not be without fault and failure when it comes to honoring their part of the covenant. Yet, God will remain faithful and committed to them, who exercise the same faith in God that Abraham did, to restore them and work with them to complete their mandate.

There are other covenants mentioned in the Bible, and there is another blood covenant between God and humanity that is extremely important to us. We will identify and discuss this blood covenant in a later chapter.

- *Takeaways for the reader:*

  - Honesty and transparency with God is not a detriment but a necessity, if we are to receive all that the Lord has in store for us

  - God's blood covenant with Abraham, and his descendants, is for all of humanity, who exercise the same faith as Abraham did, in God's faithfulness and His promises.

- *Small group questions:*

  - What keeps us from being honest with God about our questions and doubts concerning our Him and our experiences with Him?

  - What does God's blood covenant with Abraham say about God? What does it say to us, if we exercise the same faith in God as Abraham did? What can we expect from God, as a result of our faith in Him, from His blood covenant with Abraham?

CHAPTER 4

SPIRITUAL REALITIES PROPHETICALLY PRESENT

"Then the cloud covered the tent of meeting, and the glory of the Lord filled the tabernacle. Moses was not able to enter the tent of meeting because **the cloud had settled on it, and the glory of the Lord filled the tabernacle. Throughout all their journeys whenever the cloud was taken up from over the tabernacle, the sons of Israel would set out; but if the cloud was not taken up, then they did not set out until the day when it was taken up. For throughout all their journeys, the cloud of the Lord was on the tabernacle by day, and there was fire in it by night,** *in the sight of all the house of Israel."* Exodus 40:34-38 NASB (emphasis mine)

"So Moses went out and told the people the Lord's words. He assembled seventy men from the people's elders and placed them around the tent. **The Lord descended in a cloud, spoke to him, and took some of the spirit that was on him and placed it on the seventy elders. When the spirit rested on them, they prophesied,** *but only this once. Two men had remained in the camp, one named Eldad and the second named Medad,* **and the spirit rested on them.** *They were among those registered, but they hadn't gone out to the tent,* **so they prophesied in the camp.** *A young man ran and told Moses, "Eldad and Medad are prophesying in the camp." Joshua, Nun's son and Moses' assistant since his youth, responded, "My master Moses, stop them!"* **Moses said to him, "Are you jealous for my sake? If only all the Lord's people were prophets with the Lord placing his spirit on them!"** Numbers 11:24-29 CEB (emphasis mine)

God has a plan to restore humanity and the first major step to do this was enacting a blood covenant with Abraham. God communicated, demonstrated and documented His commitment to restore humanity through this covenant. He committed Himself and His resources to restore our position, purpose and authority to complete our mandate.

Humanity had been separated from God and unable to effectively relate to and interact with Him for over 2000 years, since their rebellion in the Garden. This alienation and separation had to change, and God took it upon Himself to initiate the necessary steps to bring it about. Through His covenant with Abraham, God began the long and steady process of personally revealing, instructing and mentoring humanity, generation after generation, in the truths, realities and activities associated with the Kingdom of God.

Having become almost exclusively *natural* in our orientation and focus, the spiritual world and the reality of the Kingdom of God were almost non-existent. The challenge and purpose for God's restoration is to modify humanity's orientation and what we consider to be "reality". This modification will include how humanity responds to this reality in light of our role and function as His image bearers and regents. This change in orientation and our faith-filled actions must become the "norm" for us. God created and equipped us as *natural and spiritual* beings.

Living As Natural & Spiritual Beings

When God created humanity, He placed us on the earth and gave us five physical senses, by which we encounter and interact with this natural world. These five senses help us gather intellectual information about our natural surroundings, enabling us to effectively understand and respond to it. As we receive this information from our senses, our brain processes and "rationalizes" it so we can draw conclusions and make informed decisions. These conclusions and decisions are not always accurate but, over time, we learn to trust our senses to engage, interpret and respond to this natural world, effectively.

Likewise, at our creation, God gave us spiritual "senses" by which we can effectively encounter and interact with Him and the spiritual world around us. God created us with a human spirit that resides and functions within our physical bodies. Our spirit was created to operate as the dominant "component" within our overall human experience, including our role and function within the Kingdom of God.

God equipped humanity to do something no other creature was created to do. He equipped us with the ability to *spiritually* interact with and respond to Him and the spiritual world, as we conduct our *natural* responsibilities and activities on the earth. As a result, it is our first and foremost responsibility to increase in our knowledge, understanding and experience with God and the spiritual operation of His Kingdom. God gave us a human spirit so we can recognize and engage in this spiritual relationship and activity with Him. God is Spirit, and those who desire to engage and interact with Him must do so *"in spirit and in truth"*.[45]

Our Priority of Function In This Life

As important as it is for humanity to complete our great commission, our first priority is to willingly and devotedly respond to and engage with God as those created *"in His image and according to His likeness"*, *"only slightly less than divine"*. All other human activities and responsibilities are secondary to this singularly human opportunity and privilege.

As Adam and Eve lived and ruled as God's regents on the earth, they engaged in and enjoyed direct fellowship and interaction with Him. Our *spiritual relationship* with God as His image bearers and our *natural function* within His Kingdom go hand-in-hand. This is extremely important when we consider the fact that God's throne is located in Heaven and humanity is located on Earth. Heaven is a real place and it has a specific location within the universe, just like Earth. It is critical that we be in regular communication and interaction with God so we can carry out His will and activities as if He is here ruling and governing, Himself.

Communicating, representing, governing, expanding and subduing for the Kingdom of God is our sole commission on Earth. God didn't commission us to envision and fulfill our personal dreams, visions, plans and activities for ourselves. These could be considered subversion against God, His rule, and the purpose for

---

[45] John 4:24

which we were created. This is no different than what Lucifer did when he rebelled against God and the role he was commissioned to fulfill within the Kingdom of God. If we look around us, treason and subversion are built into the very fabric of this current world's system of operation. Human governments were instituted and work hard to protect the human community against such rebellious and corrupting influences and activities. Yet, when it comes to humanity and our attitudes and actions toward God, we are engaged in these very same rebellious attitudes and activities. God wants us to share and engage in *His* dreams, visions and strategies for us because we are at our best and most fulfilled when we do.

To change our skewed orientation toward the *natural* and *corrupted*, God instructs and trains us to be more *spiritual*. We have been raised to operate by this present world's system of operation; according to our five physical senses and rational intellectualism. We have not been taught and trained to operate according to our *spirit* and the *prophetic* truths and realities of the Kingdom of God; according to our *spiritual* senses. It takes time to effectively "re-orient" our behavior from one kingdom to another. *It is a deliberate, repeatable process that God initiates within our faith experience with Him.*

God's prophetic realities originate in heaven and the impetus for its continued implementation and practical application comes from heaven. God wants us to recognize and respond to His prophetic invitations to engage and cooperate with Him in a way that is compatible with such a unique dynamic.

The Prophetic Nature & Operation of the Kingdom of God In This Age

God has compiled some of His past words, revelations and training activities in the Bible, our *covenant document* with Him. God uses the scriptures as part of our training, but it is not the sole resource He uses to reveal, instruct, train and mentor us. God, Himself, is personally and actively involved in our training and He directly delivers our training to us. *God, in heaven, delivers our training and related activities to us, here, on earth, <u>prophetically</u>, by His Spirit, in real time.*

We are going to use the terms *prophetic* and *prophetically* regularly throughout the rest of this chapter and the remainder of the book. Therefore, we are going to use the definition for *prophetic* that I provided and used in my previous book.[46]. This definition will identify and describe the manner in which God, in heaven, communicates and interacts with the earth and the people who inhabit it. If you want to learn more of this spiritual reality and dynamic, you can read about it in my previous book.

The definition we will use for *prophetic* is:

> *"The entrance of the eternal into time, the confrontation of the finite by the infinite, the intrusion of the supra-natural into the natural. The spiritual activity by which God reveals and exhibits the operation of His Kingdom within the realm of our earthly, natural existence. In essence, prophetic is the revelation of God, His Kingdom and its activities, including His wisdom, knowledge, and will, into the realm of time and our present experience. It is the thoughts and activities of God finding their expression and manifestation within the present natural world in which people live and function."*[47]

The eternal, spiritual God, and the realities and activities of His Kingdom, *prophetically* enter this natural world and engage with humanity. He encounters and influences us, by His Spirit, in order to implement and accomplish His eternal plans and purposes. This is how God relates to this world and the people in it. This is how the Holy Spirit uses the Bible and other spiritual resources to actively reveal, communicate, instruct, train and mentor humanity.

To be effective and successful, it takes an established, active and prophetic relationship between God and each individual person and faith community. This is the type of relationship God had with Adam and Eve in the Garden. This is the type of relationship God had with the children of Israel in the wilderness. This is the type of relationship God the Father had with Jesus when He was on the earth. This is the type of relationship God established in His blood

---

[46] *"Studies In The Kingdom of God"* by Tom Casey, copyright 2017, Amazon Publishing

[47] Casey, Tom. Studies In The Kingdom Of God (Kindle locations 1367-1372). Kindle Edition.

covenant with Abraham, and this is what God desires to establish with every human being.

God Prophetically Equips His People

When it came to engaging with Abraham, Isaac, Jacob, and Jacobs sons, God spoke and acted prophetically on an individual basis because His covenant people were few in number at that time. Yet, there came a time when Abraham's descendants became greater in number and God adapted accordingly. We can see this dramatic change in the book of Exodus when God expanded His training to engage His "faith community" - Moses and the children of Israel.

The descendants of Abraham, God's covenant people, had been in Egypt for 400 years. The story of Abraham's covenant with God along with other exploits their fathers, Isaac and Jacob (Israel) had experienced with God, had been passed down to them from generation to generation. Even though they knew the stories and acknowledged God as their covenant God, they knew little about Him and even less about the kind of relationship they were intended to have with Him. During their 400 years in Egypt, God's faith community had increased to nearly one million people. As they increased, the children of Israel were forced into slavery by Pharaoh and the Egyptian people out of fear that they, the Egyptians, would eventually be overrun and subjected to slavery by Israel.

Yet, the children of Israel knew enough about God to call out to Him for deliverance from this oppression and slavery. In response and in remembrance of His covenant with Abraham, God prophetically encountered a man named Moses who had been tending his father-in-law's sheep in the wilderness for decades. God invited Moses to join with Him to deliver the people from their slavery. God revealed Himself to Moses in the wilderness, as he tended the sheep, and trained him to hear and respond to Him, in faith. God trained and equipped Moses to prophetically challenge Pharaoh as His representative, as if God was standing face to face with Pharaoh, Himself. God even instructed Moses, telling him that He would *"make him as God to Pharaoh"*[48]. God further instructed Moses to speak for Him and to specifically say to Pharaoh, *"Thus says the*

---

[48] Exodus 7:1

Lord, let My people go, that they may serve Me."[49] Through Moses, God directly confronted and judged Pharaoh and Egypt.

In His promise to Abraham, God said, *"But I will also judge the nation whom they will serve, and afterward they will come out with many possessions."* God, prophetically and according to His foreknowledge, tells Abraham that *He* will judge Pharaoh and Egypt before the children of Israel come out. Yet, if we look at the scripture in Exodus, God uses His representative, Moses, to prophetically speak His words and conduct His activities that judge Egypt and bring Israel out. God's representatives and regents prophetically speak and act for God, *in His Name*, as if God is speaking and acting, Himself. They effectively represent God because they are effectively led and trained by the Spirit of God. [50] God broke the power of Pharaoh and Egypt over the children of Israel, fulfilling the prophecy He gave Abraham over 500 years earlier.

Individual Prophetic Training vs. Community Prophetic Training

Once the children of Israel left Egypt, God led His faith community on a path that would take them to the Promised Land, in a short period of time. Yet, when they arrived at the border of the land, they failed to enter it because of their doubt and rebellious unbelief in God and His instructions to them. As a result, God turned them around and led them back into the wilderness where He would engage them in His individual and community training for the next forty years.

For decades, God prepared Moses to be a shepherd and then mentored him to prophetically engage and cooperate with Him in His spiritual activities and judgments involving Egypt. God would similarly prepare and train the children of Israel, as individuals and as a "faith community", for forty years in the wilderness in order for them to enter their land of promise.

During that time, God revealed to them who He is and introduced them to the process whereby He would instruct them in the

---

[49] Exodus 8:1

[50] John 3:34; Romans 8:12-17

prophetic nature of their relationship with Him and of His divine activities. The children of Israel were God's prophetic, covenant people. As such, they had to learn how to effectively represent Him and His Kingdom to those around them. It was necessary for them to learn how to recognize, respond to, and interact and cooperate with God, effectively, as they made their way to their land of promise.

We Must Recognize and Confront The Actual Condition of Our Faith

The children of Israel didn't realize nor did they anticipate that their preparation would last forty years in that wilderness environment. They had lived in an evil and ungodly environment, with its subtly corrupting attitudes and activities, for 400 years. God knew it would take time to change their "kingdom orientation" once they were released from their slavery. Even though they acknowledged God, they did not know and understand Him. They did not know the Kingdom of God nor did they understand how to prophetically engage, interact and cooperate with Him in His spiritual activities. Changing their "kingdom orientation" would take time and would be a continual process of prophetic revelation, instruction and mentoring by God, according to His plan and with His personal oversight.

God knew the children of Israel would fail to enter the land of promise the first time He led them to its border. Yet, He led them there because they needed to recognize and confront the true condition of their faith, for themselves. They had to acknowledge their need for Him in order to successfully realize their destiny and possess what He had promised them. They did not have the *revelation* of these truths and realities, and therefore did not have the necessary *quality* of faith, the faith of Abraham, to experience them, without wavering, when His instructions came. [51] They had to see for themselves that they lacked the *proportion* of faith and *practical* spiritual experience to function effectively as God's covenant people, and to receive what He had promised them.

Within a forty-year period, God successfully changed their "kingdom

---

[51] James 1:6-8; Hebrews 10:23

orientation". He revealed Himself to a generation to embrace Him, respond to His spiritual influences and invitations, and cooperate with Him in His prophetic Kingdom activities. They experienced many successes and failures along the way, but God was able to instruct them to hear what He was saying, see what He was doing, and embrace their role and function as His faithful covenant people. He was no longer "the God of their fathers". He was their personal and ever-present God, and they were His prophetic, covenant people.

When we read Exodus through Deuteronomy, and even the book of Joshua (after they had entered the land of promise), we see times when they resembled the enemies of God rather than His covenant people. During their time in the wilderness, the subtle pagan, evil influences and practices of Egypt, which had crept into their lives, were put on full display and exposed. God had to do this so they could see for themselves how much Egypt had influenced them. Their *positional* kingdom transition took place quickly, but their *experiential* kingdom transition would take much longer.

God's prophetic instruction and preparation, *individually* and as a *faith community,* would not happen quickly. *God made the covenant with Abraham and his descendants, forever, so we would all know that He will never leave us or forsake us.* God proved to us that "*He who promised, is faithful*"! [52]

It is important for all of us, as individuals and faith communities, to recognize and accept God's invitation to be instructed and prepared by Him, and to remain engaged with Him during the restoration process. God gives us a tremendous example of why we should remain engaged with Him, in this way.

God's Covenant People Have A Choice

God created humanity with a free will; the ability to freely choose what we think, say and do. When it comes to engaging with God, we all have the ability to freely choose if and how we will respond to Him and His invitations.

---

[52] Hebrews 10:22-23

God's activities with the children of Israel in the wilderness, for 40 years, demonstrate His love for all of humanity and His desire to restore, instruct and prepare us to know Him and effectively cooperate with Him. During this 40-year period, there were times of apathy, resistance and even rebellion by the people against Him. Yet, there were also times of obedience, faithfulness and cooperation between them. They were engaged in this restoration process, together.

Tragically, there were some who willingly chose not to move forward with God's plan. They willingly chose to disengage from His process. They chose not to pursue and receive all of the benefits of the blood covenant God made with Abraham and his descendants. This sounds inconceivable, yet the scriptures tell us that it actually happened, and it has happened throughout human history.

We find a stark example of this in Numbers 32. After 40 years in the wilderness, the children of Israel were approaching the land of promise. They were finally on the threshold of entering and experiencing all that God had promised them. As we read in Numbers 32, we see the tribes of Reuben and Gad meet with Moses to make an unusual and tragic request:

> *"Now the sons of Reuben and the sons of Gad had an exceedingly large number of livestock. So **when they saw the land of Jazer and the land of Gilead, that it was indeed a place suitable for livestock, the sons of Gad and the sons of Reuben came and spoke to Moses and to Eleazar the priest and to the leaders of the congregation, saying,** "...the land which the LORD conquered before the congregation of Israel, is a land for livestock, and your servants have livestock." They said, "If we have found favor in your sight, **let this land be given to your servants as a possession; do not take us across the Jordan."***

> *"**So Moses gave command concerning them** to Eleazar the priest, and to Joshua the son of Nun, and to the heads of the fathers' households of the tribes of the sons of Israel. **Moses said to them, "If the sons of Gad and the sons of Reuben, everyone who is armed for battle, will cross with you over the Jordan in the***

presence of the LORD, and the land is subdued before you, then you shall give them the land of Gilead for a possession." [53]

We also see that half of the tribe of Manasseh chose to join the tribes of Reuben and Gad in remaining in the land of Gilead. These 2½ tribes elected to not enter their inheritance; the land God promised them. In their minds, the land they had previously conquered as part of God's restoration process and prophetic training seemed to sufficiently satisfy their needs, as they perceived them. As far as they could tell, based on their own personal perception and understanding, the land of Gilead, outside of the land of promise, was sufficient for them. When asked by Moses concerning their request, God responded that it was ultimately their choice to enter the land, or not.

These tribes had spent nearly forty years with the rest of the children of Israel, experiencing the prophetic presence and activities of God, as He revealed and conducted them. They had progressed through His restoration process, trained and mentored by God to live in His presence and cooperate with Him in His Kingdom activities.

These 2½ tribes evaluated themselves, including their possessions and the community status they had acquired over the years. Based on this, they decided that their present location and circumstances, though outside of the land of promise, was sufficient to satisfy them and their needs, moving forward. They were short-sighted. To them, entering and possessing the land of promise wasn't necessary. They chose to disengage from God's training and restoration process. Why would they do this?

A person could reason that if these tribes were content to settle their families, possessions, and livestock outside of the promised land, why not do so? They could settle in and put down roots as individuals, families, and as a "faith community". That doesn't seem like an unreasonable way to look at the situation except for one thing; the dynamic presence of God and His prophetic training activities would no longer be with them. God was moving forward with the rest of His covenant people, into the land of promise. For

---

[53] Numbers 32:1-5, 28-32   NASB   (emphasis mine)

these 2½ tribes, life, as they had known it, would not be the same; it couldn't be. They still loved God and God still loved them. They would attempt to continue living according to the Kingdom training they had received up to that point. Yet, the dynamic, prophetic presence of God would move forward without them.

Did God abandon them? No. They were free to choose what they would do. God will not force Himself, His promises, or His prophetic instruction upon anyone. Nor, will their decision to remain behind deter God from accomplishing His divine plans and activities. God is not obligated to save, deliver, restore or fulfill by many or by few. [54] God was going to lead His people to enter and possess their inheritance.

In the scriptures and throughout Church history, God has shown, time and time again, that He will, if necessary, accomplish His plans and activities with a relatively few number of people. The few may not have a theology that is impeccable (who's is?). They will be weak, flawed people. God, from the beginning, has chosen to engage and work in cooperation with individuals and faith communities, regardless of their number.

God's divine plans and prophetic training activities may seem "unorthodox" or "questionable" to our human reasoning and accepted religious and theological "norms". In fact, they may very well offend us if we trust too much in our "natural" abilities, intellectual prowess or religious "sensibilities". God is looking for our faith, the faith of Abraham, and willing cooperation.

God had prepared so much more for these 2½ tribes, if they had only continued to engage with and follow Him all the way to the *promise; their inheritance*. There was so much ahead of them that they missed, that they didn't even know existed, because they didn't stay engaged with God all the way.

The writer of the book of Hebrews puts it this way:

> *"But without faith it is impossible to [walk with God and] please Him, for whoever comes [near] to God must*

---

[54] 1Samuel 14:1-15

[necessarily] believe that God exists and that He rewards those who [earnestly and diligently] seek Him." [55]

There is a *diligent resolve* and an *expectation of reward* that is essential to seeking and knowing God and staying engaged with Him. We must diligently follow God with the expectation and faith that, doing so, will produce the results God has promised us. *We must not abandon our earnest expectation of reward if we are to diligently continue our passionate pursuit of God and His inheritance for us.*

We should not forget that God loves all of us, passionately. He exercises abundant grace and patience with us because He knows our weakness. As a result, He doesn't give up on us if we don't recognize or initially respond to His invitations to join Him in His prophetic training. God will continue to influence us and invite us to join Him. He may directly invite us through prophetic impressions, dreams and visions, or He may invite us, indirectly, using other individuals. God never gives up on us. Yet, the more we refuse or resist His invitations, the more difficult it becomes to positively respond to Him the next time He invites us.

God loved these 2½ tribes; they were His chosen, covenant people. He did not give up on them after they initially decided not to move forward with His dynamic, prophetic presence into the Promised Land. After the warriors within these 2½ tribes fought with the other 9½ tribes to help them enter and possess the Land, they made their way back to the land of Gilead, across the Jordan River, where the rest of their people had settled. Before they crossed the river, God once again invited them to enter the land of promise and possess their inheritance within it. God made the invitation by speaking to them through a man named Phinehas, inviting them to join the other 9½ tribes, if they had changed their mind. Yet, the 2½ tribes chose to remain in Gilead, outside of their inheritance, the land of promise.[56]

So, what ever happened to the tribes of Reuben, Gad, and the half-tribe of Manasseh? The Bible doesn't tell us what happened to them. In fact, no one seems to know what happened to them. There

---

[55] Hebrews 11:6 Amplified Bible

[56] Joshua 22:13-31

seems to be no mention of them in history books and no mighty works of God documented in regard to their activities, after they stayed behind. God doesn't want this to be our legacy and outcome.

A Visible, Complete and Reliable Example

I mentioned earlier that there is another blood covenant enacted between God and humanity that is very important to us. In addition, God has given humanity a living, complete and reliable example of how a Kingdom regent is to function and what that relationship with God is to look like, in its purest form. Adam and Eve did not maintain their relationship for very long before they rebelled against Him. The example of the children of Israel gives us a glimpse of what this relationship can look like and accomplish. Yet, it falls short of giving us a clear and reliable example, and its desired results.

In the next chapter, we will look at this other significant blood covenant, as well as this complete, reliable and living example of what the regency role and relationship with God is to look like. We only get a 3½-year view, but it is a tremendous revelation and opportunity to see it function, as God intends.

- *Takeaways for the reader*:

  - God has created humanity to effectively engage and interact with two realms of reality, the *natural* and the *spiritual*. Each individual within the human family is created with five physical senses to encounter and interact with the natural world, and spiritual senses (a human spirit) to engage and interact with the spiritual world.

  - God, in heaven, and His spiritual Kingdom engage and interact with humanity, on the earth, *prophetically*. To effectively interact and cooperate with God and His Kingdom activities, we must learn how to engage and function, prophetically.

o God wants to prophetically instruct and prepare us, as *individuals* and as a *faith community*. There are examples we can observe and learn from, in God's restoration process and training of the children of Israel.

o We all, as individuals and faith communities, have a choice to engage with God's prophetic Kingdom training, and how long we will stay engaged with it. If we don't stay engaged, we can miss out on promises He has given us.

• *Small group questions*:

o God created humanity to engage and interact with two realms of reality, the *natural* and the *spiritual*. Identify and discuss the reasons why we are much better at engaging and interacting with the natural world. Identify and discuss what we can do to better engage and interact with the spiritual world. What are your conclusions?

o God prophetically engages, interacts and trains His covenant people to know Him and to cooperate with Him in His Kingdom activities. This takes a willing heart and time, to accomplish. What are the *similarities* between what God did to reveal, prepare and train Moses, individually, and what He did with the children of Israel, as a faith community? What are the *differences*?

o In God's restoration process and training for us, there are, both, milestone achievements and difficult roadblocks on our journey. Discuss and identify some of these milestone achievements and roadblocks. How does God use all of them to accomplish in and through us, what He has planned and promised? What can we do to stay engaged with Him, and not settle for a faith experience *outside of the land of promise*?

CHAPTER 5

FIXING OUR EYES AND FOLLOWING OUR EXAMPLE

"...let us run with endurance the race that is set before us, fixing our eyes on Jesus, the author and perfecter of faith, who for the joy set before Him endured the cross, despising the shame, and has sat down at the right hand of the throne of God." Hebrews 12:1-2 NASB (emphasis mine)

"Have this attitude in yourselves which was also in Christ Jesus, who, although He existed in the form of God, did not regard equality with God a thing to be grasped, but emptied Himself, taking the form of a bond-servant, and being made in the likeness of men." Philippians 2:5-7 NASB (emphasis mine)

We have a God who loves us so much that He has sworn, by Himself, to do what we are incapable of doing for ourselves, in order to help us complete the great commission He gave us at our creation!

As our covenant God, His words and activities are focused on; 1) revealing Himself and His divine nature to us; 2) personally restoring, instructing and mentoring us; and 3) giving us a demonstrated and reliable example of what our relationship and activities with Him are to look like and produce.

Yet, there is an important reality in regard to our relationship with God that must be confronted and resolved. It is the required execution of humanity's death sentence, resulting from our rebellion and treason against God in the Garden.

Jesus of Nazareth: Humanity's Sinless Substitute

Humanity's relationship with God and our understanding of Him was on a steady decline after our rebellion in the Garden. Beginning with Abraham, God instructed and mentored humanity in the truths and realities of who He is and the operation of His Kingdom, so we can eventually be restored. Yet, there was an *elephant in the room* that could not be ignored and was impeding our ultimate success; it must be resolved.

God's righteous judgment upon humanity's rebellion must be executed and finalized. This was the ultimate requirement for humanity if we are to work in total, undivided unity and cooperation with God from a pure and willing heart.

God is the Supreme Judge of the universe. As such, He could not allow humanity's treason to go unpunished, no matter how much He loves us and wants us to complete what we started. In a completely righteous, legal and eternally binding act, God initiated what theologians refer to as a *Penal Substitutionary Atonement*.

This occurs when a fellow human being willingly and legally submits himself to the court as a sacrificial substitute for the guilty party's lawless offense. This legal substitute is to receive and suffer the full weight of the court's justice and judgment for the offense, on the guilty party's behalf. In order to present himself as this legal substitute, this person must be found personally innocent of the same lawless offense; he must be guiltless in the court's eyes.

As this relates to humanity and our rebellion against God, every single human being since Adam and Eve's sinful act has been guilty of this same act of treason. How can an innocent, guiltless person be presented as a legal substitute for humanity, if *"all have sinned and fallen short of the glory of God"*? [57] Enter, the human being, Jesus of Nazareth.

Jesus was a fully human being, born of a virgin by the power of God.[58] As a result, He was born guiltless and remained guiltless for His entire life. Jesus never rebelled against or disobeyed God the Father during His life. He willingly presented Himself to the Father as humanity's sinless substitute. He willingly took the guilt and shame of our treason upon Himself and surrendered His body and shed His

---

[57] Romans 3:23
[58] Matthew 1:18-25

blood in His just execution by God, upon the cross. As a result, God declared Jesus' execution "acceptable" for humanity's punishment, completely freeing humanity from their guilt, shame and penalty of death, forever. This complete and eternal atonement for humanity's treason is available to anyone who humbly and willingly turns back to God, in faith, and identifies with Jesus in His death, burial and resurrection. Every person who does this is spiritually "born again" to newness of life.[59]

The New Covenant In Jesus' Blood

At the same time Jesus presented Himself to the Father as humanity's sinless sacrifice, He enacted a universal and perpetual blood covenant with the Father, on humanity's behalf. This blood covenant, between the Father and Jesus (humanity), declared once and for all that humanity's guilt and shame was completely and eternally judged and our death sentence, served. The debt humanity owed to God is paid in full. The scriptures refer to this covenant as the *New Covenant,* in Jesus' blood:

> *"And when He had taken some bread and given thanks, He broke it and gave it to them, saying, "**This is My body which is given for you**; do this in remembrance of Me." And in the same way He took the cup after they had eaten, saying, "**This cup which is poured out for you is the new covenant in My blood**."* [60]

Paul, in his letter to the Roman believers, describes this sacrificial atonement and blood covenant that Jesus enacts with the Father, and how all of humanity is set free from the guilt of treason, through faith in Jesus' sacrifice:

> *"**This righteousness is given through faith in Jesus Christ to all who believe**. There is no difference between Jew and Gentile, for all have sinned and fall short of the glory of God, and **all are justified freely by his grace** through the redemption that came by Christ Jesus. **God presented Christ as a sacrifice of**

---

[59] Romans 6:3-7
[60] Luke 22:18-20 NASB (emphasis mine)

*atonement, through the shedding of his blood—to be received by faith. He did this to demonstrate his righteousness, because **in his forbearance he had left the sins committed beforehand unpunished— he did it to demonstrate his righteousness at the present time**, so as to be just and the one who justifies those who have faith in Jesus."* [61]

God righteously and legally dealt with the *elephant in the room,* in His own way and in His own timing! Now, the cryptic prophecy that God spoke to Satan in the Garden was fulfilled. The seed of the woman has crushed Satan's head. Satan has been eternally defeated and his authority over humanity has been stripped from him by Jesus' resurrection from the dead. The power of sin and death over humanity has been broken.[62] Humanity can, now, move forward to fulfill our role as God's regents and to complete our mandate. The guilt and shame of our treasonous act, that has been holding us back, has been completely absolved. The authority to rule and subdue the earth has been restored to humanity, in Jesus.

All authority to rule and subdue the earth has been given to the human, Jesus, the son of David, our Savior. Possessing this authority, Jesus has delegated the exercise of it, on the earth, to His human followers. With this powerful Kingdom resource, we are to carry out the will and purposes of God on the earth, and to complete our mandate as God's image bearers and regents.

The Regency Relationship & Role Personified

Now, with redeemed humanity having received this delegated authority from Jesus, as His followers and earthly representatives, this exposes another weakness and need that we have. As a result of sin and its effect upon us, our relationship with and knowledge of God, and our position and role as His image bearers and regents, has deteriorated to the point where we are functioning almost exclusively as *natural, soulish* beings. Our orientation and approach to God, the earth, and our place within creation is not what God desires and intends for us. We know and understand

---

[61] Romans 3:22-26 NIV (emphasis mine)
[62] Romans 8:1-2

very little of our *spiritual* orientation and our relationship and role with God.

To be reliable and effective representatives for the Kingdom of God, we need a real-life depiction of what this *spiritual* orientation is to look like, how it integrates with our *natural, soulish* orientation, and how our role and relationship with God is to truly function. We need a living example that we can watch, listen to and emulate.

The example of Moses and the children of Israel in the wilderness is very helpful because it shows us the challenges involved when flawed human beings work their way through God's restoration process and prophetic training. Other examples in the Old Testament were, likewise, flawed and unreliable models. Yet, God wants us to know what it should look like so we can *"be imitators of God"*,[63] working in cooperation with the power and presence of the Holy Spirit.[64]

Kingdom Discipleship

God began His restoration process with humanity by prophetically inviting and engaging with *individuals.* As the number of His covenant partners increased, God's scope and methods for engaging, inviting and training them changed. God adapted in order to be effective on a *community* scale. Both of these distinct yet complimentary trainings were on full display in God's dealings with the children of Israel, in the wilderness, for forty years. Both are important and the intended outcome is basically the same. Yet, *the prophetic training for the individual is intended to end with their physical death, while the prophetic training for the faith community is intended to continue, in perpetuity.*

God prophetically engages with an individual, which leads to their inclusion in the faith community and their prophetic training. As both trainings move forward, together, they "feed" each other, contributing to their mutual growth and maturity. When an individual "leaves" the community training, God intends for their role and function to continue. This is accomplished when another

---

63 Ephesians 4:30-5:2
64 Romans 8:14

individual "steps in" to fill that role, and the faith community keeps moving forward and maturing. When individuals are not effectively trained and mentored to prophetically step into these roles, the individual and faith community can be effectively "stalled" or may even decline in their ability to progress toward spiritual maturity. [65]

The death or other manner of loss of a mature, vibrant member of God's faith community and prophetic training is costly in His sight because of the potential setback this can create in our overall efforts to mature and progress. Even within the functional, yet flawed, examples of God's prophetic training at work in scripture, we can see the influence, growth and results these inter-personal and inter-generational relationships can experience and generate. These prophetic relationships that God initiates and engages in with His covenant individuals and faith communities is what I call *Kingdom Discipleship*.

> Kingdom Discipleship: *God's use of dynamic, practical and lasting prophetic relationships and encounters, with individuals and faith communities, initiated and empowered by the Holy Spirit. The purpose is to reveal, instruct, train and mentor in the spiritual realities relating to the person and nature of God, and the prophetic nature, presence and activities of His Kingdom. It is to utilize inter-personal and inter-generational mentoring relationships in order to effectively strengthen the individual and, thereby, the entire faith community. The goal is to present every individual and the entire faith community to God; skilled, accomplished and mature.*

This Kingdom Discipleship is what God describes to us in Ephesians 4, where Paul writes:

> *"He gave some apostles, some prophets, some evangelists, and some pastors and teachers.* **His purpose was to equip God's people for the work of serving and building up the body of Christ until we all reach the unity of faith and knowledge of God's Son. God's goal is for us to become mature adults—to be fully grown, <u>measured by the standard of the fullness of</u>**

---

[65] Ephesians 4:14-16

Christ. *As a result, **we aren't supposed to be infants any longer** who can be tossed and blown around by every wind that comes from teaching with deceitful scheming and the tricks people play to deliberately mislead others. Instead, by speaking the truth with love, **let's grow in every way into Christ**, who is the head. The whole body grows from him, as it is joined and held together by all the supporting ligaments. The body makes itself grow in that it builds itself up with love as each one does its part.*" [66]

God prophetically invites and engages the individual, and the faith community, in His Kingdom training, by His Spirit. God works, in cooperation with the prophetic community, to: *1) equip God's people to faithfully participate and deliver His desired results, according to His divine plan; 2) instruct, train and mentor each member of the faith community until we function as a complete unit; 3) enable His people to faithfully relate to and prophetically cooperate with God as His regents; 4) know Jesus, and to embrace the full scope of His example to us of faithfulness, obedience and maturity; and 5) attain to the fullness of Jesus' example, as our standard of measure.*

Jesus of Nazareth: The Reliable Example of Our Regency Relationship With God

Jesus' personal relationship with the Father and His prophetic ministry and discipleship activities with His followers is our reliable, demonstrated example of what humanity's regency relationship with God is to look like and produce, in its purest form!

Jesus was, is, and always will be God. Yet, for 33 years, He emptied Himself of (or laid aside) His privileges as God; His non-communicable attributes as God (being all-knowing, all-powerful, ever-present, etc.) to live His life as a fully human being. Jesus lived His life and conducted His ministry activities as a human who was led and empowered by the Holy Spirit [67]. Jesus' faithfulness to His relationship and role with the Father enabled Him to remain

---

[66] Ephesians 4:11-16 CEB (emphasis mine)

[67] Luke 3:21-22; Luke 4:1,14-15

completely obedient and sinless His entire life, until His sacrificial death and blood covenant with the Father could be justly accomplished and enacted.

By sending Jesus to personify and accomplish these things, the Father was being faithful to His blood covenant with Abraham. God was engaging in the necessary activities to help us where we were incapable of helping ourselves. Jesus spent time prophetically demonstrating, instructing and training His followers in God's Kingdom realities and activities. This included what our relationship with God was to look like and produce. Jesus engaged in *prophetic discipleship* with His followers, empowered by and cooperating with the Holy Spirit.

For over three years the Father and Jesus demonstrated to us the dynamics of this relationship's unity, cooperation, activities and results that God created humanity to experience with Him. *What the Father desired to communicate, demonstrate and accomplish regarding Himself and His Kingdom culture and activities, Jesus accomplished in the Father's name, as if the Father was here saying and doing these things, Himself.* God desires and intends for us, as His new covenant people, to learn from, conduct and accomplish these same things, following Jesus' example. In John 17, when Philip asked Jesus to show or demonstrate the Father to them, Jesus responded by saying:

> *"Have I been so long with you, and yet you have not come to know Me, Philip?* **He who has seen Me has seen the Father;** *how can you say, 'Show us the Father'? "Do you not believe that* **I am in the Father, and the Father is in Me?** *The words that I say to you* **I do not speak on My own initiative, but the Father abiding in Me does His works.** *"Believe Me that* **I am in the Father and the Father is in Me; otherwise believe because of the works themselves.** *"Truly, truly, I say to you,* **he who believes in Me, the works that I do, he will do also; and greater works than these he will do;** *because I go to the Father.* **"Whatever you ask in My name, that will I do, so that the Father may be glorified in the Son.** *"If you ask Me anything* **in My name, I will do it.""** [68]

70

Jesus is telling His disciples that He has been the Father's visible, reliable example and representative to them, saying what the Father wants to be said, demonstrating who the Father is, and carrying out the Father's prophetic activities for the entire time He was with them. Jesus is our living, reliable example of what all of humanity was created to be and do, in the beginning. Philip and the other disciples didn't recognize it because the earth and humanity had been so long without such a faithful and competent example. *They were looking with such anticipation for God's Kingdom and promised Messiah that they didn't recognize God's faithful and obedient Regent standing right in front of them!*

Jesus used regency relationship language when He said:

> "*I do not speak on My own initiative, but **the Father abiding in Me does His works**. "Believe Me that **I am in the Father and the Father is in Me**...*"

The Father was in Jesus, communicating His words and accomplishing His works as if the Father was here doing them, Himself. Jesus was "in" the Father, *prophetically* hearing what the Father was saying and seeing what the Father was doing. The Father was "in" Jesus, *prophetically* speaking what He wanted to say and doing what He wanted to do. Jesus *prophetically* carried out the communication and demonstration activities of the Father, by faithfully listening to and following the Holy Spirit. *This is the regency role and relationship at work! This is how God created humanity to live.*

Yet, Jesus didn't stop there, when He responded to Philip's request. He went on to say:

> "*Truly, truly, I say to you, **he who believes in Me, the works that I do, he will do also; and greater works than these he will do; because I go to the Father**. "Whatever you ask in My name, that will I do,* so that the Father may be glorified in the Son. "If you ask Me anything **in My name**, I will do it.*"

---

[68] John 14:9-14 NASB (emphasis mine)

Jesus elaborated by saying that *those who believe in Him and follow His example of devoted faith and willing obedience to God, can walk in this same regency relationship and these same prophetic activities and realities.* Not only that, Jesus tells us that we will engage in *even greater prophetic Kingdom activities* than He did *because He is going to the Father.*

Jesus tells the disciples that He would be going back to the Father, in Heaven, in order to send the Holy Spirit upon those of the human family who willingly choose to follow Him and His example. These devoted followers would be sent throughout the world to communicate and conduct these same and even greater prophetic activities, as the Father's regents empowered by the Holy Spirit.

Jesus goes on to describe what else is included in this relationship dynamic, by saying:

> *"Whatever you ask **in My name, that will I do,** so that the Father may be glorified in the Son. "If you ask Me anything **in My name, I will do it.**"*

The True Unity of the Faith

When Jesus was engaged and cooperating with the Father, they acted as one and spoke as one. They were engaged *as a complete unit.* When Jesus prayed and asked the Father for something, the Father gave it to Him because Jesus was not asking in order to accomplish His own agenda and for His own wants and ambition. Jesus was asking it as the Father's representative and to accomplish the Father's will.

Jesus tells His followers that if they remained *in unity of purpose and activities with Him and the Father,* they could ask for anything they would need to accomplish those activities and He would give it to them, *so that the Father would be glorified in the Son.* God's regents are to be one with the Father and Jesus just as Jesus was one with the Father. They will act as one and speak as one, in unity, together. When we are united with the Father and Jesus in this way and act on Their behalf, based upon this unity of desire and purpose, the Father and Jesus will be glorified in what we do. *This is the unity of the faith!*

Jesus confirms this, in John 17, when He prays to the Father for all of those who will follow Him:

"I glorified You on the earth, having accomplished the work which You have given Me to do. Holy Father, keep them in Your name, the name which You have given Me, that they may be one even as We are. As You sent Me into the world, I also have sent them into the world. I do not ask on behalf of these alone, but for those also who believe in Me through their word; that they may all be one; even as You, Father, are in Me and I in You, that they also may be in Us, so that the world may believe that You sent Me. The glory which You have given Me I have given to them, that they may be one, just as We are one; I in them and You in Me, that they may be perfected (completed, restored) *in unity, so that the world may know that You sent Me, and loved them, even as You have loved Me."* [69]

All of humanity was created to experience the same unity of relationship and activity with God that Jesus, the Holy Spirit, and the Father experienced, together, when Jesus was here! *As willing participants in this same relationship, we are to ask Jesus and the Father for whatever we need, to speak what God is saying and demonstrate what God is doing, as if He was here doing it, Himself.* Jesus tells us that the Father will answer our prayers, giving us whatever we need, as He answered Jesus' prayers!

Not, only, are we to experience and demonstrate the same prophetic works that Jesus did; we are to experience and demonstrate even greater works than He did because He would send the Holy Spirit upon us, as the Father sent the Holy Spirit upon Him. *To be complete in unity, as Jesus prayed, we must be united with Jesus and the Father in thought and purpose, allowing them to speak and demonstrate their will through us, as their regents and representatives; that we may be in unity with each other and with Them, even as They are in unity with each other.*

---

[69] John 17:18-26 NASB (emphasis and parenthetical mine)

This is God's goal. We must be prophetically trained and mentored in these truths and realities just as Jesus was, by the Father and the Holy Spirit, and as Jesus prepared His disciples. The Holy Spirit is here to do just that, as we engage with and follow Him.

As we accept God's invitation to engage in this training, individually and as faith communities, there is a unique "twist" we should be aware of. Jesus faithfully lived His life and carried out His activities as Regent and Messiah because of His love for the Father, His will, and His purposes. Yet, even as Jesus faithfully carried out His Kingdom activities, He knew that the Father had wonderful things in store for Him, as a result of His faithfulness. There was a reward in store for His faithfulness that helped motivate Jesus during His earthly life. Likewise, God has rewards for us that are to help motivate our faithfulness during our earthly lives. Let's find out more about this often-overlooked Kingdom reality.

Jesus' Earnest Expectation Of Reward

When Jesus, God in the flesh, was here on earth as one of us, He lived His life to accomplish the Father's will, not His own. He set Himself to be led by the Holy Spirit. Jesus lived His life, conducted His ministry, and engaged in prophetic discipleship with His followers by the power of the Holy Spirit.[70] He endeavored to speak, respond, and take action in all things as the Father would, if the Father was here, Himself.

Much like the children of Israel in the wilderness, Jesus lived with promises from the Father; an earnest expectation of successful completion and reward; His "land of promise" *in this life.* This expectation was five-fold: 1) to faithfully and accurately *reveal* the Father's nature and character to us; 2) to fully *communicate* and *demonstrate* the Father's will and activities to us; 3) to *willingly* and *fully* bear the guilt and divine judgment of humanity's treason, upon Himself; 4) to *break* Satan's authority and *defeat* the power of sin and death over humanity; and 5) to *produce* prophetic disciples of the Kingdom of God who will continue to expand His ministry and extend the message and activities of the Kingdom of God to the entire world.

---

[70] Luke 4:1-2,14-21

As the Gospels and other New Testament writings so clearly communicate and describe to us; as followers of Jesus, we are to be an extension and the continuation of Jesus' regency role and activities with the Father, upon the earth, to the entire earth, and in each generation. Like Jesus, this is *our* earnest expectation of successful completion and reward; our "land of promise" *in this life.* This is *the Great Commission* that Jesus was engaged in while He was on the earth, and this is *the Great Commission* we are engaged in while we are upon the earth. The Great Commission is more than proclaiming the good news of Jesus's death, burial, and resurrection to all of humanity. *It is to proclaim and demonstrate the power and presence of the Kingdom of God upon the earth, as its witnesses and God's regents.*

Therefore, we must engage in a life-long, diligent pursuit to engage with and be prophetically trained by the Holy Spirit. This requires an earnest expectation of successful completion and reward. Jesus engaged in this diligent pursuit and God has given us tremendous incentives to follow Jesus' lead and to stay engaged. While giving Jesus and us tremendous incentives to engage in our diligent pursuit *in this life*, God also gave Jesus, and has given us, a "hope of reward" *beyond this life.* The writer of Hebrews encourages us with this, by telling us:

> *"Therefore, since we have so great a cloud of witnesses surrounding us, **let us also lay aside every encumbrance and the sin which so easily entangles us, and let us run with endurance** the race that is set before us, **fixing our eyes on Jesus**, the author and perfecter of faith, **who for the joy set before Him endured the cross, despising the shame, and has sat down at the right hand of the throne of God.**"* [71]

Paul gives us more insight concerning this earnest expectation of reward, when he tells us:

> *"**Have this attitude** in yourselves **which was also in Christ Jesus**, who, although He existed in the form of God, did not regard equality with God a thing to*

---

[71] Hebrews 12:1-2 NASB (emphasis mine)

*be^jgrasped, **but emptied Himself**, taking the form of a bond-servant, and **being made in the likeness of men**. Being found in appearance as a man, **He humbled Himself by becoming obedient to the point of death**, even death on a cross. **For this reason** also, **God highly exalted Him, and bestowed on Him the name which is above every name, so that at the name of Jesus** EVERY KNEE WILL BOW, **of those who are in heaven and on earth and under the earth, and that every tongue will confess that Jesus Christ is Lord**, to the glory of God the Father." [72]*

Not only did Jesus sit down at the right hand of the Father, as the 2nd Person of the Trinity, He sat as King and Lord of all humanity and of the earth.[73] Jesus was already King of the universe, as God, but now He was also King and Lord of humanity and the earth, as a human. Jesus didn't stop being human when He ascended into heaven. Jesus will forever rule all of creation as God, and He will lead and rule the affairs of earth and humanity, as a human. When the Father gave Jesus THE name which is above every name, every name must and will bow its knee to Him and confess Him as King and Lord. This was Jesus' expectation and hope of reward.

As the people of God and Jesus' representatives on the earth, we have a similar promise and hope of reward *beyond* this life. As we will discover in greater depth, in a later chapter, we, too, will rule as kings in the age to come. Paul encourages us with this truth when he says:

> *"It is a trustworthy statement: For if we died with Him, we will also live with   Him; **If we endure, we will also reign with Him**; If we deny Him, He also will deny us; If we are faithless, He remains faithful, for He cannot deny Himself." [74]*

Jesus also confirms this, when He declares to His followers at the Church at Laodicea:

---

[72] Philippians 2:5-11 NASB (emphasis mine)

[73] 1Timothy 6:13-15; Revelation 17:14; Revelation 19:16

[74] 2Timothy 2:11-13 NASB (emphasis mine)

*"He who overcomes, **I will grant to him to sit down
with Me on My throne, as I also overcame and sat
down with My Father on His throne.**"* [75]

There is a resoluteness and diligence involved with following the
Holy Spirit and engaging with His prophetic training, throughout
our lives. God is restoring us in order for us to complete our
mandate. We can now look at the relationship and activities that
Jesus enjoyed and participated in with the Father and the Holy
Spirit, and see what humanity was intended to have and enjoy with
God when He created us. God still wants us to enjoy and experience
relationship with Him, as we move forward toward completing our
great commission.

The Level Playing Field

In Isaiah 53, the prophet Isaiah describes the "natural" attributes
the Messiah (Jesus) would possess, when He came. Isaiah tells us:

*"**He has no** (stately) **form or majesty that we should
look upon Him, nor appearance that we should be
attracted to Him.**"* [76]

There was nothing about Jesus' birth, societal status or physical
appearance that would inspire anyone to give Him a second look,
when it came to recognizing and honoring Him as the coming
Messiah. He was not born in a palace. He wasn't physically
attractive. Nor, did He display the kingly honor or grandeur you
would expect from the Son of God.

Yet, when Jesus engaged with the Father to embrace what was being
communicated and revealed to Him, He willingly chose to
implement the Father's will and agenda, not His own. Jesus'
willingness to obediently communicate and conduct the Father's
business is what attracted the people to Him. *It wasn't Jesus'
vibrant personality and good looks that attracted people; it was
the character qualities and prophetic activities of God being
displayed in and through His life that attracted them.*

---

[75] Revelation 3:21 NASB (emphasis mine)
[76] Isaiah 53:2 NASB (emphasis mine)

As a result, the Holy Spirit empowered Jesus to accomplish wonderful, prophetic works of the Kingdom of God, in the Father's name.[77] *This truth removes any pretense we may have that a person must have a vibrant and engaging personality, a specific social or economic status, a certain level of education or religious standing, or an attractive physical appearance to be a successful, useful representative of the Kingdom of God.* Jesus, fully and obediently representing and demonstrating the Father's character qualities and prophetic activities, is our reliable, complete example of what our regency relationship with God is to look like and accomplish.

God has established the key, foundational elements of what is necessary for humanity to successfully accomplish our mandate. He defeated the power of Satan, hell and death through the death, burial and resurrection of Jesus. Likewise, He has given us documented, written instructions (the Scriptures) and a reliable, comprehensive relationship example to follow in the life and ministry of Jesus. To top it off, God has given us the personal, indwelling presence of the Holy Spirit to lead, instruct, train and mentor us in His prophetic training. This is all vitally important to us as we move forward with God's individual and community training, in the years ahead.

- *Takeaways for the reader*:

  o Jesus willingly became humanity's substitute for God's just judgment upon our rebellion and treason against Him, so we can be restored to God, our role and function as image bearers and regents, and to complete our mandate.

  o Jesus and the Father enacted another blood covenant, in Jesus' blood, that sealed humanity's place and destiny in God's Kingdom order, forever. Humanity is restored to their relationship with God and role and function as

---

[77] John 17:6-12

image-bearers and regents, through their identification with and faith in Jesus' death, burial and resurrection.

o God has given humanity a visible, reliable model and example of what the regency relationship between God and humanity is to look like and accomplish, in its purest form, through Jesus life and ministry

o Jesus showed us what God's *prophetic discipleship* is to look like, how it is to operate through the presence and power of the Holy Spirit, and what it is to accomplish in and through the lives of individual followers of Jesus and the faith community

o We are to pursue our relationship with God and His prophetic training with an urgent expectation of reward, *in* this life and *beyond* this life, as Jesus did when He was here.

- *Small group questions*:

  o Jesus is our visible, reliable example of what humanity's relationship with God is to look like and accomplish.

    ▪ How do we discover, recognize and understand what Jesus' relationship example entails and is to accomplish, so we can follow His example and experience some of those same results?

    ▪ What part does the Holy Spirit play in this regency relationship?

    ▪ How do we recognize and respond to the Spirit's invitations to engage with Him in this relationship, as Jesus did?

  o Jesus engaged His followers in the Holy Spirit's *prophetic discipleship*, as individuals and as a faith community. Jesus instructed, demonstrated, trained, and mentored His followers in these prophetic Kingdom realities and activities.

- How did the Holy Spirit lead, participate and operate within Jesus' life and ministry activities?

- What did Jesus do to respond to and cooperate with the Holy Spirit, to see these prophetic Kingdom realities and activities occur in His life and ministry?

- What did Jesus do to instruct, demonstrate, train and mentor His followers so they could respond and cooperate with the Holy Spirit, as He did, in these prophetic Kingdom realities and activities?

CHAPTER 6

IMAGE BEARERS EQUIPPED, TRAINED AND MENTORED BY GOD

"For a person is not a Jew who is one outwardly, and true circumcision is not something visible in the flesh. On the contrary, **a person is a Jew who is one inwardly**, *and* **circumcision is of the heart—by the Spirit**, *not the letter.* **That man's praise is not from men but from God.**" Romans 2:28-29 HCSB (emphasis mine)

"Peter stood with the other eleven apostles. He raised his voice and declared, "Judeans and everyone living in Jerusalem! Know this! Listen carefully to my words! These people aren't drunk, as you suspect; after all, it's only nine o'clock in the morning! Rather, **this is what was spoken through the prophet Joel: 'In the last days, God says, I will pour out my Spirit on all people. Your sons and daughters will prophesy. Your young will see visions. Your elders will dream dreams. Even upon my servants, men and women, I will pour out my Spirit in those days, and they will prophesy. I will cause wonders to occur in the heavens above and signs on the earth below**, *blood and fire and a cloud of smoke. The sun will be changed into darkness, and the moon will be changed into blood,* **before the great and spectacular day of the Lord comes. And everyone who calls on the name of the Lord will be saved.**""" Acts 2:14-21 CEB (emphasis mine)

Redeemed humanity is in an eternal relationship and partnership with God! We are partners in two perpetual blood covenants with Him: 1) the Abrahamic Covenant, and 2) the New Covenant in Jesus' blood. For Abraham and his blood-line descendants (the Jewish people) to participate in God's covenant promises, physical circumcision was the "mark" or sign of commitment to the covenant. For Jesus' followers, the Church, to participate in God's New Covenant promises, "circumcision of the heart", the New Birth by the Holy Spirit, is the "mark" or sign of commitment to the covenant.

To participate as a partner in either blood covenant, a mark or sign of commitment to the covenant is to be made – circumcision; one, a physical circumcision and the other, a spiritual circumcision. The question is, are we required to be a participant in both covenants, and their related circumcisions, to be partners with God and beneficiaries of the promises of the covenants? The answer is, "no", and Paul explains to us why we don't:

> *"For circumcision benefits you if you observe the law* (the Law of Moses), *but if you are a lawbreaker, your circumcision has become uncircumcision. Therefore, if an uncircumcised man keeps the law's requirements, will his uncircumcision not be counted as circumcision? A man who is physically uncircumcised, but who fulfills the law, will judge you who are a lawbreaker in spite of having the letter of the law and circumcision. For a* **person is not a Jew who is one outwardly,** *and* **true circumcision is not something visible in the flesh.** *On the contrary,* **a person is a Jew who is one inwardly,** *and* **circumcision is of the heart—by the Spirit,** *not the letter.* **That man's praise is not from men but from God.**" [78]

The initial "mark" of the Abrahamic covenant was physical circumcision. God implemented physical circumcision as a temporary faith response because humanity was spiritually incapable of true, complete faithfulness to God and His covenant. Sin's damaging effect upon the human heart made complete faithfulness to God in thought, word and deed, impossible. Physical circumcision was to be a visible "mark" or reminder of the covenant, and a sign of the person's desire and intent to be faithful to God and the covenant. It was an outward "type" or symbol of the "true" circumcision that was to come; the inward circumcision of the heart – a permanent transformation of the human spirit, by grace through faith.

Jesus served humanity's death sentence for rebellion and treason

---

[78] Romans 2:28-29 HCSB (emphasis mine)

against God and enacted the New Covenant with the Father. As a result, individual members of the human family can be "born again". With the "new birth", the human spirit is transformed (circumcised) by the Spirit of God and humanity's internal, spiritual condition is restored to its original condition, by God's grace. Humanity can become covenant partners with God, participating in the promises of the covenant, through the individual's identification with and faith in Jesus' substitutionary death and resurrection.

The new "mark of the covenant" is the "New Birth", by the Holy Spirit. Physical circumcision is no longer necessary or adequate. The promises and conditions of the New Covenant are even greater than what was promised under the Abrahamic covenant.[79] The Abrahamic covenant and its promises were not annulled by the New Covenant. The New Covenant fulfilled the Abrahamic covenant and expanded the covenant promises available to those who choose to become covenant partners with God, through Jesus Christ. As a result, God has provided everything we need to enjoy a strong and meaningful relationship with Him and to accomplish our mandate.

Jesus received all authority, in heaven and on earth, when He ascended into heaven, after defeating Satan and stripping him of the authority he stole from humanity in the Garden.[80] The New Covenant partner is immediately transferred from the domain of darkness to the Kingdom of God.[81] No longer are they slaves to sin, Satan and his authority. They are, now, servants of righteousness and of God.[82] They are restored to their position as image bearers within the Kingdom of God and receive the authority to act as God's regents on the earth, once again.

Jesus gives this authority to every New Covenant partner, once they receive the new birth. Jesus accomplished the will of the Father with the authority given to Him by the Father, by the power of the Holy Spirit.[83] These New Covenant partners are to exercise this same authority, by the power of the Holy Spirit, to accomplish the will and activities of God. We are to do these things, *in Jesus' name.*[84]

---

[79] Hebrews 8:6; 2Peter 1:1-4

[80] Matthew 28:18-20

[81] Colossians 1:13

[82] Galatians 4:6-7

[83] John 17:4; Luke 4:1,14-21

We Are Witnesses Of The Presence Of The Kingdom Of God

Jesus told His disciples that He was sent by the Father to proclaim and demonstrate the presence of the Kingdom of God in all the cities to which He traveled.[85] Prior to Jesus leaving the earth, He told His disciples that before the end of the age, the good news of the presence of the Kingdom of God would be proclaimed throughout the world, *as a witness* to all peoples and nations, and then the end would come.[86] What does Jesus mean, "as a witness"? In my previous book, I spend time discussing this and want to highlight a key statement, here, because it gives us a clear understanding of what it means and what it should look like when we proclaim the Kingdom of God, *as a witness*:

"When Paul neared the end of his life and he was being held under house arrest, he continued to preach the Kingdom of God to those who came to him. When Jesus was teaching His disciples about the things that would take place before His return to the earth at the end of the age, He told them that this gospel or good news of the Kingdom of God must be proclaimed as a witness. This word witness (Greek. marturion) means to observe and experience something first-hand and to give testimony to its reality. In other words, to be a witness of the Kingdom of God we must observe and experience its reality first-hand in our lives and be able to demonstrate and give personal testimony to that reality.

If we don't have that first-hand experience and observation, we aren't witnesses; we are simply giving hearsay testimony based on what we've heard from others, who may or may not have experienced it. How can I demonstrate and give testimony as an eyewitness of something that I haven't observed or personally experienced? As we will see, the Kingdom of God is to be observed, personally experienced, and its reality

---

[84] John 17:11-12,18,20-26; Mark 16:17-20

[85] Luke 4:42-43

[86] Matthew 24:14

demonstrated by the followers of Jesus. Otherwise, there is no real testimony of its reality and presence." [87]

Before Jesus' return, God's earthly regents will walk in a greater level of spiritual reality, authority and prophetic activity than ever before. God wants the peoples and nations of the earth to hear the message of the Kingdom of God and to witness its presence and power, firsthand. Jesus tells us this will happen, when He says:

> *"He said to them, "Go into all the world and preach the gospel to all creation. Whoever believes and is baptized will be saved, but whoever does not believe will be condemned. And **these signs will accompany those who believe: In my name they will drive out demons; they will speak in new tongues; they will pick up snakes with their hands; and when they drink deadly poison, it will not hurt them at all; they will place their hands on sick people, and they will get well."** After the Lord Jesus had spoken to them, he was taken up into heaven and he sat at the right hand of God. Then the disciples went out and preached everywhere, and **the Lord worked with them and confirmed his word by the signs that accompanied it."** * [88]

Peter, in the book of Acts, also declares this reality when he quotes the prophet Joel, on the Day of Pentecost:

> *"Peter stood with the other eleven apostles. He raised his voice and declared, "Judeans and everyone living in Jerusalem! Know this! Listen carefully to my words! These people aren't drunk, as you suspect; after all, it's only nine o'clock in the morning! Rather, **this is what was spoken through the prophet Joel: 'In the last days, God says, I will pour out my Spirit on all people. Your sons and daughters will prophesy. Your young will see visions. Your elders will dream dreams. Even upon my servants, men and women, I will pour out my Spirit in those days, and they will prophesy. I***

---

[87] Casey, Tom. *Studies In The Kingdom Of God: 2 Volumes In 1 Book* (Kindle Locations 373-385). Kindle Edition.

[88] Mark 16:15-20 NIV (emphasis mine)

will cause wonders to occur in the heavens above and signs on the earth below, blood and fire and a cloud of smoke. The sun will be changed into darkness, and the moon will be changed into blood, before the great and spectacular day of the Lord comes. And everyone who calls on the name of the Lord will be saved."" [89]

Before we move forward to discuss the meaning of these scriptures, I want to address some confusion in the Body of Christ related to this previous scripture from Mark 16. Many followers of Jesus believe this scripture is questionable, regarding its authenticity and validity, because of the note attached to it by modern Bible translators. The note states that these verses do not appear in the earliest manuscripts of the gospel of Mark that have been discovered. For this reason, many Bible scholars and teachers suggest that we may disregard this portion of Mark 16.

There are two important reasons why we *can* and *should* take these verses from Mark 16 as the word of God and covenant promises from Him: 1) there are similar scriptures in the other gospels where Jesus made the same basic promise to His disciples;[90] and 2) we can find examples of what Jesus said would take place, in these particular verses in Mark 16, being experienced and fulfilled in the book of Acts. [91] The remaining gospels and the book of Acts bear witness and confirm that what Jesus said would take place in Mark 16:15-20 are, indeed, God's word and should be believed and trusted as His covenant instructions and promises to us.

There is an important point I want to make here, as we briefly look at the miracles, signs and wonders of the Kingdom of God that will occur in the period leading up to "the time of the end" and the return of Jesus to Earth. We find that many of God's prophetic activities, which occurred in the book of Acts, did not, first, occur in the Old Testament or in the gospels as part of Jesus' ministry.[92] There was no "biblical precedence" for them before they occurred. Likewise, there are examples of God's prophetic activities occurring

---

[89] Acts 2:14-21 CEB (emphasis mine)

[90] Luke 10:17-19; Matthew 10:5-8

[91] Acts 16:16-18; Acts 2:4; Acts 10:44-46; Acts 28:1-6; Acts 3:1-10

[92] Acts 8:26-40; Acts 9:10-16; Acts 10:9-16; Acts 11:27-28; Acts 12:6-10 – to name a few

in the Old Testament that do not, subsequently, occur during Jesus' ministry as described in the gospels, or through His disciples in the book of Acts. God's future prophetic activities were not limited to what He had conducted in the past.

Are we to limit God and our spiritual experiences with Him to only those activities that have a "biblical precedence"; that only appear in the gospels, or Acts, or even the Old Testament? *The purpose of the Bible, including the New Covenant writings, is not to put God and humanity in a "theological box", declaring that only those prophetic activities that appear in the Bible are valid for us and our experience today, thereby limiting God's ability to work in and through His people as He desires.*

The purpose of the New Covenant is to free humanity from our slavery to sin and Satan, and to equip and empower us to engage with God. We are free to do whatever He wants us to do, whenever He wants us to do it, as if God was here doing these things, Himself. God knows what He wants to do, when He wants to do it, and for whom He wants to do it. All we have to do is engage and cooperate with Him so He can conduct these prophetic activities through us.

We should not put artificial or theological constraints on God or us. If God wants to say or do something, we, as His representatives, should be open and available to cooperate with Him to accomplish it, *in His name. "For all who are being led by the Spirit of God, these are sons of God."* [93] We should expect and anticipate that God will engage us, and the Holy Spirit will lead us, in this way as we conduct God's desired activities, on His behalf. *We are here to accomplish God's will, not the other way around.*

For instance, before Jesus ascended into heaven, He gathered His disciples around Him to instruct them, one last time:

> *"Gathering them together, He commanded them not to leave Jerusalem, but to **wait for what the Father had promised, "Which," He said, "you heard of from Me.**"* [94]

---

[93] Romans 8:14 NASB

[94] Acts 1:4 NASB (emphasis mine)

Jesus had previously revealed and instructed His disciples in a spiritual reality and activity, and He was, now, reminding them that this activity was going to occur soon, and how to prepare for and respond to it.

On the Day of Pentecost, when the Holy Spirit was poured out on the disciples and the people in Jerusalem, Peter, seeing what was happening, remembered what Jesus had taught them. He was prepared to cooperate with the Holy Spirit, in the event. Peter, in his message to those in attendance that day, proclaimed:

> *"...these men are not drunk, as you suppose, for it is only the third hour of the day; but **this is what was spoken of through the prophet Joel...".**[95]*

When Peter stood up to speak that day, he simply communicated the information concerning this event, that Jesus had taught them before He left. Jesus had taught His disciples concerning this scripture in Joel 2; what it was referring to and that it would be fulfilled, shortly. This declaration by Peter and the information he conveyed to the people that day, didn't just "appear out of thin air". Peter and the other disciples were instructed, trained and mentored by Jesus concerning it, and were, therefore, able to recognize it and cooperate with the Holy Spirit when it occurred. Peter may not have known everything that was going to happen that day, and what the results were going to be, but he knew enough to recognize what was happening and was able to cooperate with the Holy Spirit, in it.

Prophetically Equipped & Trained By The Holy Spirit

God, the Holy Spirit, is in His new covenant partners, continually, to lead, reveal, mentor, and guide us. This prophetic activity is to occur throughout this present age, culminating with the return of Jesus at the end of the age. Joel foretold this and Peter declared:

> *"Even **upon my servants, men and women, I will pour out my Spirit in those days,** and they will prophesy. **I will cause wonders to occur in the heavens above and signs on the earth below,** blood*

---

[95] Acts 2:15-16 NASB

*and fire and a cloud of smoke. The sun will be changed into darkness, and the moon will be changed into blood, **before the great and spectacular day of the Lord comes**. And everyone who calls on the name of the Lord will be saved.'"*

"The great and spectacular day of the Lord" refers to the return of Jesus to the earth, as its King, to establish the visible Kingdom of God. The prophetic activities of God are to continue through the hands of Jesus' followers throughout *the time of the end,* culminating with tremendous wonders and signs occurring by God's hand, shortly before Jesus returns. God continues to instruct and train us to cooperate with Him in these prophetic activities, so we can partner with Him in their implementation, until the end of the age.

God has given humanity a "Kingdom blueprint" with over sixty years of documented examples, including their results, for how this prophetic training is to operate, what it is to look like, and what it is to produce within the New Covenant faith community (the Church). This blueprint is what we call the New Testament. Throughout the gospels, Jesus gives us instructions, supplies us with prophetic examples, and encourages us regarding future events and outcomes. Through their letters and a chronological journal of apostolic and prophetic events and activities, the apostles and other early-Church leaders expand on Jesus' instructions. They increase these instructions according to divine revelation, document additional and more varied prophetic examples, and provide encouragement through additional insight into future events and outcomes.

Additionally, the New Testament writers instruct and demonstrate to us how we can mature in our ability to imitate and represent Jesus, throughout the earth and in every generation. When Jesus left the earth to return to heaven, He gave gifts to His prophetic faith community in order to equip and prepare us to continue His mission and ministry. These gifts are to equip and support us to be God's physical mouths, hands and feet, as we are trained by the Holy Spirit through His prophetic training. *Through the instructing and mentoring leadership of these gifts, and by prophetic example, each individual and faith community is to participate and mature in God's training as we progress to complete our divine mandate.* Paul puts it this way:

> *"I, the prisoner of the Lord, implore you to* **walk in a manner worthy of the calling with which you have been called...to each one of us grace was given <u>according to the measure of Christ's gift</u>**. *Therefore it says,* "WHEN HE ASCENDED ON HIGH, HE LED CAPTIVE A HOST OF CAPTIVES, AND **HE GAVE GIFTS TO MEN.** "...*And* **He gave some as <u>apostles</u>, and some as <u>prophets</u>, and some as <u>evangelists</u>, and some as <u>pastors</u> and <u>teachers</u>, <u>for the</u> equipping of the saints for the work of service, <u>to the</u> building up of the body of Christ;** <u>until we all attain to</u> **the unity of the faith**, *and of* **the knowledge of the Son of God, to a mature man, <u>to</u> the measure of the stature which belongs to the <u>fullness of Christ</u>**...*speaking the truth in love,* **we are to grow up in all aspects into Him who is the head, even Christ**, *from whom the whole body, being fitted and held together by what every joint supplies, according to the proper working of each individual part,* **causes the growth of the body for the building up of itself in love.** " [96]

The purpose of these "ascension gifts" of Jesus is to:
- equip the saints for the work of service

- buildup of the body of Christ

The goal of the work of these "ascension gifts" is that:
- we all attain to the unity of the faith

- we all attain to the knowledge of the Son of God

- we all attain to a mature man, to the measure of the stature which belongs   to the fullness of Christ

To attain to these goals, for God's prophetic training, *"grace has been given"* to each follower of Jesus, *"according to the measure of*

---

[96] Ephesians 4:1-16 NASB (emphasis mine)

Christ's gift".[97]

The Measure of Faith & Our Proportion of Faith

For the followers of Jesus, there is another *elephant in the room* and it can best be stated with a question, *"Now that redeemed humanity has been saved and brought back into the Kingdom of God, are we expected to prophetically demonstrate this same reliable and complete representation of God's character, words and activities as Jesus did, since we have been corrupted by sin and its results?"*

As I mentioned before, the *new birth* brings the immediate transition and re-orientation of our human spirit, from the domain of darkness to the Kingdom of God. Our spirit is in perfect relationship with God so that we can effectively communicate and interact with Him at any time and in any place. Our physical body still bears the results of sin and must be transitioned to an eternal body, which will happen, instantly, at a single point in time in the future. Yet, it is the transition and re-orientation of our soul (our mind, emotions and will) that takes time and continues to be clouded and hindered by sin and its results, throughout our lifetime. Our soul must be transformed and restored, and this doesn't happen immediately. This re-orientation of the soul is the key to our ability to effectively mature and function within our regency relationship and role with God, in this life.

Paul gives us some insight and practical understanding concerning our ability to re-orient our soul and effectively mature and function as God's image-bearers and regents, in this life:

> *"Therefore I urge you, brethren, by the mercies of God, to present your bodies a living and holy sacrifice, acceptable to God, which is your spiritual service of worship.* ***And do not be conformed to this world, but be transformed by the renewing of your mind, so that you may prove what the will of God is, that which is good and acceptable and perfect*** *(complete). For through the grace given to me I say to everyone among you not to think more highly of himself than he ought to think; but to think*

---

97 Ephesians 4:7

*so as to have sound judgment, **as God has allotted to each a measure of faith**. For just as we have many members in one body and **all the members do not have the same function**, so we, who are many, are one body in Christ, and individually members one of another. **Since we have gifts that differ according to the grace given to us**, each of us is to exercise them accordingly...according to the proportion of his faith."* [98]

Paul puts things in perspective for us concerning our ability to reliably and completely represent God's character, words and activities. In this present age, God gives each of us, as followers of Jesus, "*a measure of faith*". God also gives *gifts* to each of us, by the Holy Spirit, according to His grace, based on His eternal plan and at His discretion. Each of us is to *exercise* these gifts, as is appropriate for each gift, "*according to the proportion of his faith*"; according to the *level* of faith we have developed for each gift. *The measure of faith God gives to each of us is to be exercised. As this faith is exercised in each gift, we grow and mature in our ability to function in these gifts according to the proportion of our faith that we have developed, throughout our training.*

The Holy Spirit is present with us to reveal, instruct, train and mentor us as we exercise our measure of faith with these gifts. Yet, it is our responsibility to *desire earnestly*[99] to know what our gifts are and to exercise them, by continually *asking, seeking* and *knocking*[100]. We are to increasingly exercise faith in our gifts in order to grow and mature in the *proportion* of faith it takes to exercise them at greater and greater levels. The Holy Spirit won't do it for us, but He is with us, to help us, as we respond to Him within our prophetic Kingdom training. Let me explain what I mean by giving you an example from my own personal faith experience with God's prophetic training.

A Personal Example

---

[98] Romans 12:1-6 NASB (emphasis mine)

[99] 1Corinthians 14:1

[100] Matthew 7:7-11

After coming to know Jesus and being born again at the age of 18, I eventually became involved with the youth ministry at a local Presbyterian church, and became a volunteer Young Life leader at a local high school. Later, I was asked to join the summer youth staff at the church for that next summer. I didn't know a lot about the Bible, but I was growing. I didn't realize it at the time, but God had engaged me in His prophetic training and I had already experienced several prophetic encounters, which I didn't understand and didn't know how to process.

This Presbyterian church had purchased two neighboring homes and used them for the youth ministry. As a male member of the summer youth staff, I and several other young men were asked to live in one of these homes for the summer. The entire youth staff met during the day for Bible study and training, and conducted middle school, high school, and college/career ministry activities in the evenings and on weekends. I slept in the basement of one of the houses, with two other male staff members.

As a volunteer Young Life leader, I met a lot of students from the high school I was assigned to, as they attended the weekly meetings and other events we sponsored. As a result, many of them took part in the youth activities of the Presbyterian church, over the summer. During this first year as a Young Life leader, I met a young man who was having a difficult time. He was involved with "white" magic, was taking illegal drugs, and was often dealing with suicidal thoughts. I'll refer to this young man as "Joe", even though this wasn't his real name. Joe had attended some Young Life meetings, even though he was inconsistent and hung around on the periphery of the activities. I got to know Joe a little bit and when summer came, he got similarly involved with the summer youth activities at the church.

One night, several of us were sitting around the house talking and Joe happened to be there. We could tell Joe was getting sleepy, so we invited him to stay over and sleep in the basement with us, on the couch. He took us up on the offer.

Joe, I, and another male youth leader went downstairs to get some sleep. The other youth leader (I'll refer to him as "Pete" even though this wasn't his real name) and I weren't tired enough to go to sleep, but Joe went to sleep on the couch, almost immediately. Sometime later, as Pete and I were continuing to talk, suddenly I experienced something I hadn't experienced before. Inside of me, my core, I "sensed" the presence of evil and this evil seemed to be growing in intensity, as if it was getting closer and closer. It wasn't fear; there was nothing to be afraid of. It was as if pure evil was present, right there. This was a "fleeting" experience in that I only experienced it momentarily. I didn't know what this was about or what to think.

At the same time I was experiencing this "awareness" of the presence of evil, Pete and I could see Joe getting restless and agitated on the couch. He started mumbling as if he was having a dream or a nightmare. Pete suddenly spoke in Joe's direction, saying, "Leave him alone." After 2-3 seconds, we heard Joe say, with a deep, sinister and defiant voice, "No, he's mine." Pete and I looked at each other. This was not Joe speaking. We looked back at Joe and he still looked like he was asleep, but he was breathing hard and agitated. Then, Pete said, "What is your name?" The voice from Joe responded, "There are many of us."

Pete and I looked at each other again, realizing what was happening. We found ourselves in the presence of demons, who were harassing Joe and speaking to us. Pete shrugged his shoulders and said, "Well, let's do this." We got our Bibles and sat down in front of Joe. I didn't know what to do, hoping that Pete did. As we sat down and began to silently pray, Joe opened his eyes and faced us. Even though it was Joe facing us, it wasn't Joe looking at us or speaking to us. We were speaking with demonic forces.

As we sat there, Pete did most of the talking, as I prayed, silently, next to him. As I prayed, a unique language of prayer, that I did not recognize, arose within me. I knew it was God, so I did my best to articulate this prayer language, silently, as I sat in front of Joe. Suddenly, Joe looked over at me and said, "Stop that; we don't like that." I wasn't praying out loud, but the spiritual force of my prayers was having a noticeable effect on them. Hearing this, I prayed all the more fervently. They pleaded with me to stop. We asked them how many there were. They responded that there were nine of them. We commanded them to come out of Joe, in the name of Jesus, and not to bother him again. Shortly, they came out of him and he slumped back on the couch, looking like he was asleep.

When Joe opened his eyes, Pete and I talked with him for a few minutes and explained to him what had happened. We explained to him that he needed to heartily pursue a relationship with Jesus and to renounce the "white" magic and stop using the drugs, as these activities gave the demons an entrance into his life, to harass him. We prayed with Joe to commit his life to Jesus. If there was any question in my mind about the reality of the spiritual realm, it was answered that night. Spiritual beings, such as angels and demons, actually do exist.

This was a specific prophetic training the Holy Spirit invited me into. As I responded, He engaged with me, and Pete, to help us work our way through the experience, and to help Joe find freedom from this demonic harassment. Yet, this wasn't the end of God's prophetic training for me, in this area. I had begun to exercise *the measure of faith* He had given me but I didn't realize at the time that there was a "gift", a spiritual manifestation[101], that He had given me and was beginning to train and develop within me.

Over the next few years, I had several prophetic experiences similar to this first one. Each was a little different from the others, but the purpose and outcomes were the same. Each time, I experienced an initial 'sense" of the presence of evil. I knew God was teaching me something, but I wasn't quite sure what it was.

As time passed, I experienced several unique encounters, as I slept. It is important to understand and be aware that while we sleep, our body is resting but our mind and spirit remain active. As a result, the Holy Spirit often engages with us while we sleep because our soul (mind, emotion, will) and body are not actively engaged in the natural, daily activities taking place around us. These daily physical and mental activities can distract us and "mask" such divine, prophetic communication activities. It may take a few nighttime encounters for us to recognize and respond to this spiritual reality. God will use these prophetic methods (dreams, visions, impressions, revelations) to communicate with us and train us.

During these encounters, as I slept, deep within me, in my core, I suddenly became aware of the presence of evil, in varying degrees. I recognized these experiences as being similar to what I encountered

---

[101] 1Corinthians 12:4-11

with Joe and Pete. As I remained asleep, that same language of prayer rose up within me and I prayed the words in my mind. I continued to pray until the evil presence went away. Then, I would wake myself up.

As I reflected on these experiences, I knew they were prophetic encounters designed by the Holy Spirit to instruct and train me. It was evident that my spiritual praying, in the presence of these evil spirits, caused them to leave. But it was my next prophetic encounter that enabled me to understand what the Holy Spirit was endeavoring to teach me.

One night, as I slept, deep within my core, I became aware of the presence of holiness; of good. This time, I forced myself to wake up. When I did, I lifted my head and looked around the room. As I looked toward the bedroom door, I saw what looked like a very tall man standing just inside the doorway of the bedroom. He had a glow around him; he was "encased" in light. I knew this was an angel. After looking at him for several seconds, he disappeared.

As I lay in bed, reflecting on this and the other prophetic encounters, it seemed as if God was allowing me to distinguish between what the presence of evil and the presence of good "felt" like. He was "inviting" me into a spiritual reality as well as instructing and training me in its operation and results. God was revealing to me a spiritual manifestation (gift) that He had given to me. It is what the scriptures refer to as the *discerning* (distinguishing) *of spirits*.[102] By the enabling of the Holy Spirit, I was able to spiritually "sense" or "feel" the presence of these spirit beings and to distinguish between the presence of good (the angel) and the presence of evil (the demons). This *distinguishing* was taking place within my spirit. It wasn't an intellectual, emotional, or physical experience but a spiritual one. I had already become aware of and gained understanding of the spiritual prayer language He gave me. It is an important spiritual and prophetic tool in the operation of this manifestation of the discerning of spirits, that He has given me and was training me in.

This spiritual manifestation isn't the "gift of discernment", which is a common misunderstanding among Christians. I'm not able to

---

[102] 1Corinthians 12:10

engage in this gift whenever I want to but only as the Holy Spirit enables me to experience it. Now that I recognized and understood what He was doing, I could embrace it as an invitation and gift from God, for me. Now, I can cooperate with the Holy Spirit in order to *come into agreement with Him* concerning how He wants to implement and use this gift in my faith experience with Him, for His glory and for the common good.

This is one example of what the spiritual operation of the Kingdom of God and a manifestation of the Spirit can "look" like, within our faith experience. This is God's prophetic training at work. It would have been beneficial for me to have had someone within my faith community who understood and had experienced similar spiritual manifestations and encounters. I could have gone to them for insight, instruction, training and mentoring, in my desire to understand and grow in this spiritual manifestation, much earlier in my experiences with it. This is one of the reasons why *Kingdom Discipleship* is so important within the faith community.

I have experienced and exercised both of these spiritual manifestations many times over the years. In regard to the distinguishing of spirits, most of the time I don't actually encounter or engage with the spirits, but I am aware they are present and influencing people or the environment near me. In these situations, I engage with my prayer language to ask the Lord what it is He wants me to know about the presence of the spirits, good or evil. Occasionally, it is the presence of angels as they "minister to the needs of the saints".[103] At other times, the Spirit reveals that there are evil spirits present, often motivating and influencing the spiritual environment or, even, a specific individual or a group of people near me. There is always a reason why these or other manifestations of the Spirit are operating in me, and I seek the Lord for the reason and how I should respond.

This is just one example of how God can invite us into and engage with us in His prophetic activities. He has given all of us spiritual manifestations (gifts), by the Spirit, when we are born again. Then, He will engage with us; inviting us to participate in specific prophetic encounters and experiences in order to reveal them to us, as well as to instruct and train us in their implementation and

---

[103] Hebrews 1:13-14

operation. It is important for us to be available, aware, sensitive and responsive to the Holy Spirit when He encounters us. Otherwise, we can miss the invitations and prophetic opportunities when they come.

We Know In Part & Prophesy In Part

Yet, when it comes to our ability to function in these spiritual manifestations and operations, at the same level that Jesus did when He was here, Paul instructs us:

> **"For we know in part and we prophesy in part;** but when the perfect comes, the partial will be done away."
> **"For now we see in a mirror dimly,** but then face to face; now I know in part, but **then I will know fully** just as I also have been fully known."* [104]

God wants all of us to encounter, experience, learn and mature in our spiritual manifestations and gifts. That is what His prophetic training is for, and why the Holy Spirit is here. We are to grow in our ability to respond to and cooperate with God in His spiritual activities, as His image bearers and regents. We are to speak and act as God would, if He was physically here to do it, Himself. We choose whether we will respond and engage with Him, or not. It is our choice, as free-will beings. He will not force us. He will take us as far as we are willing and committed to go.

Paul goes on to explain, in 1Corinthians 12:10, that the followers of Jesus will prophetically "hear" and "see" what God is doing in a *partial* or *incomplete* manner, in this age, until Jesus establishes the physical, complete Kingdom of God on the earth, upon His return. This is due to, 1) the Kingdom of God is present but "hidden" or "veiled"; it operates prophetically in this age; 2) sin's effect upon our souls and bodies. We have been transferred from the domain of darkness to the Kingdom of God. We are in the midst of a kingdom "re-orientation", much like Moses and the children of Israel experienced when they left Egypt and set out for the land of promise. We are in the process of being restored, as image bearers

---

[104] 1Corinthians 13:9,10,12 NASB (emphasis mine)

and regents, and it takes time for God's prophetic training to accomplish its results, in and through us.

God is able to conduct this present and ongoing restoration process and training as long as we choose to stay engaged with the Holy Spirit, our teacher, trainer and mentor. We don't want to be like the 2½ tribes of Israel, who chose to end their journey and settle in a land that was outside of their inheritance. We don't want to be satisfied with what we have, thinking that it is enough for us. The dynamic presence of God and the spiritual activities of His Kingdom are moving forward, to bring us into the "land of promise"; to restore us and help us to complete our mandate.

The Essential Purpose Of The Ascension Gifts Of Jesus

God has given to each of us "*the measure of faith*". This "measure" of faith is the "*measure of Christ's gift*" that Paul is talking about in Ephesians 4. We receive this *measure* of faith when we are born again and we are to continue exercising it, increasing and developing our *proportion* of faith until it matures[105] and we attain to these goals that Paul identifies for us. In addition to exercising our faith to attain to these goals, we are to exercise our faith in the spiritual manifestations and operations (gifts) we have been given, by the Holy Spirit. We are to continue exercising our faith until we attain to the *maturity* of faith that Jesus possessed and demonstrated when He was here; just one aspect of *the fullness of Christ*.

We have talked about the *goals* of God's prophetic training but what do these "ascension gifts" (apostle, prophet, evangelist, pastor, teacher) of Jesus have to do with achieving them? They are *critical* to our success. The proper focus and function of these ascension gifts is essential to the faith maturation and spiritual manifestation (gift) demonstration of God's covenant people. We should be able to observe the *maturation* level of *the proportion of faith* and the *demonstration* level of the *manifestations of the Spirit* within the faith community of Jesus as a gauge of the effectiveness of these ascension gifts. Why? Because, according to Paul, this is the *purpose* of these gifts:

---

[105] Romans 12:6

- to equip the saints for the work of service

- to build up the body of Christ

What does it mean to *"equip the saints for the work of service"*? What does it mean to *"build up the Body of Christ"*? In my previous book I spent some time explaining the responsibilities and necessary activities of these ascension gifts. One excerpt from the book I want to include here explains what the purpose for these ascension gifts is within the faith community:

> *"In this scripture, there are two activities that Paul mentions; 1) "the equipping of the saints for the work of service", and 2) "the building up of the body of Christ". The individual members of the Body of Christ are to be engaged in activities designed to equip them for the work of Kingdom service, and to build them up in their Christian faith. What does this mean, to "equip"; to "build up"?* **To "equip", means to "provide a complete furnishing, supplying or endowing". To "build up", means "to promote, stimulate and support another's growth". So, the activities Paul talks about are to, 1) "provide a complete furnishing, supplying and endowing to each member of the Body of Christ for the purpose of Kingdom service; and, 2) to promote, stimulate and support each member's faith and spiritual growth".** [106]

This is the singular commission and essential responsibility of the ascension gifts of Jesus. They, too, as individual followers of Jesus, should exercise their faith and demonstrate their spiritual manifestations just as other followers of Jesus are encouraged to do. Yet, this, alone, is not proof of their commission as an ascension gift. Stephen exercised his faith and his spiritual manifestations at a very high level, performing mighty miracles among the people. Yet, he was not an ascension gift but was chosen as one of several individuals to serve food and wait on tables at the community meals.[107]

---

[106] Casey, Tom. Studies In The Kingdom Of God: 2 Volumes In 1 . Kindle Edition.

[107] Acts 6:1-6

The New Testament does not tell us that an ascension gift's directive is to, simply, "preach" and exercise one's divinely assigned spiritual manifestations. All followers of Jesus are commissioned to do this. Before He ascended into heaven, Jesus mandated and encouraged His eleven remaining apostles to implement this very commission for all believers.[108]

Jesus' commission of the apostle, prophet, evangelist, pastor and teacher; the ascension gifts of Jesus, is to provide a complete furnishing, supplying and endowing of God's Kingdom truths and realities to every follower of Jesus. This involves training, mentoring and supporting them in their prophetic service to the Kingdom of God, and promoting, stimulating and supporting the exercise and growth of their "measure of faith". By doing so, the "proportion of faith" of the individual, as well as the entire faith community, will effectively grow and mature. Throughout the world and in every generation, until Jesus returns, the ascension gifts are to establish and maintain a prophetic Kingdom culture within the faith community of Jesus, and to instruct, train and mentor the community in the Kingdom truths, spiritual realities and prophetic activities associated with the presence of the Kingdom of God.

This is what Jesus did, as our example, while He was here. As THE regent and representative of the Father and the Kingdom of God to humanity, He proclaimed and demonstrated the presence of the Kingdom of God, as a witness to this reality. As THE Apostle, Prophet, Evangelist, Pastor and Teacher, Jesus instructed, trained, mentored and supported His disciples in their efforts to experience this reality and demonstrate it with spiritual manifestations and operations, by the Holy Spirit. This is how the ascension gifts of Jesus are to function within the faith community of Jesus, and what they are to produce, in His name, as if Jesus was here doing these things, Himself.

The Manifestations of the Spirit

In 1Corinthians 12-14, Paul instructs us concerning the *manifestations* of the Spirit; the "grace gifts" that are distributed to

---

[108] Mark 16:14-18

all of the followers of Jesus and function by the ability of the Holy Spirit. God has equipped the Church with these prophetic resources and tools so we can carry out His spiritual activities on the earth, as His representatives, as if God was here doing these things, Himself. Paul tells us:

> "Now **there are varieties of gifts**, but the same Spirit. And **there are varieties of ministries**, and the same Lord. **There are varieties of effects, but the same God who works all things in all persons**. But **to each one is given the manifestation of the Spirit for the common good**. For to one is given **the word of wisdom** through the Spirit, and to another **the word of knowledge** according to the same Spirit; to another **faith** by the same Spirit, and to another **gifts of healing** by the one Spirit, and to another **the effecting of miracles**, and to another **prophecy**, and to another the **distinguishing of spirits**, to another **various kinds of tongues**, and to another **the interpretation of tongues**. But **one and the same Spirit works all these things, distributing to each one individually just as He wills**." [109]

There are a variety of *gifts*, a variety of *ministries* and a variety of *effects* (manifestations) that are included in the spiritual resources and weapons God has equipped His people with, by the Holy Spirit. *All* followers of Jesus have been equipped with them. Paul tells us that each follower of Jesus has received at least one of these spiritual *effects* or *manifestations*, by the Holy Spirit, for the common good.

These spiritual manifestations were not new to humanity when they were given to the Church on the Day of Pentecost, in the outpouring of the Holy Spirit. Spiritual manifestations had been seen and experienced by the people of God in the Old Testament and in the ministry of Jesus. In contrast to their mass distribution on the day of Pentecost, they were usually conducted in the Old Testament, one person at a time, usually by the prophets. Likewise, spiritual manifestations were conducted in the ministry of Jesus, by the Holy Spirit. *God's covenant people, including Jesus when He was on the earth, have always been prophetic people because their god is the*

---

[109] 1Corinthians 12:4-11 NASB

living God and their relationship and interaction with Him is a prophetic relationship, when accompanied by faith.

Let's take a look at these manifestations of the Holy Spirit as they were experienced by Jesus and the early-Church believers. We, as followers of Jesus in every generation, are commissioned to engage in and continue His ministry,[110] as if Jesus was here doing it, Himself. As a result, He has given us these manifestations of the Holy Spirit to enable and empower us to do just that. Here are just a few examples, being conducted by Jesus and the early Church believers:

- *The Word of Wisdom*:
  - Luke 4:23-27; Matthew 25:31-46; John 4:15-24; Acts 2:25-33; Acts 27:21-26

- *The Word of Knowledge*:
  - John 1:47-51; John 21:18-19; Matthew 24:9-13; Matthew 26:17-19; Acts 9:10-16; Acts 16:9-10

- *Faith*:
  - Matthew 14:15-21; Matthew 14:25-32; Luke 5:4-7; Mark 8:22-26; Acts 28:1-5

- *Gifts of Healings*:
  - Mark 1:30-31; John 4:46-47; Mark 1:40-45; Luke 17:11-19; Acts 3:4-8

- *Working of Miracles*:
  - John 2:1-11; Luke 5:1-11; Luke 7:11-18; Matthew 8:23-27; Matthew 14:15-21; Acts 5:12-16; Acts 5:19-21; Acts 8:4-8; Acts 8:39-40; Acts 12:6-10

- *Prophecy*:
  - John 12:31-32; John 1:26-34; Matthew 24:4-8; John 7:37-39; Acts 13:1-3

- *Distinguishing of Spirits*:

---

[110] John 17; Mark 16:14-20; Acts 1:6-8

- Mark 1:23-28; Matthew 8:28-34; Matthew 16:21-23; Acts 13:6-12; Acts 16:16-18

- *Various Kinds of Tongues & Their Interpretation*:
  - Acts 2:3-4; Acts 10:44-48; Acts 19:6

The purpose of these and other manifestations of the Spirit have always been for God's people to confirm and demonstrate the presence and ability of God. They should not be shunned, ignored, explained away or relegated to a bygone era. They are God's provision and handiwork that testify to His existence, character, and engagement in the affairs of humanity. They display the reality and presence of His Kingdom on the earth. Therefore, they are to be coveted, embraced, pursued and experienced by all of God's people. Jesus is our example of what we are to do, how we are to do it, and what the results of such prophetic activities are to accomplish, *in His name.*

As Jesus instructed and mentored His disciples in these spiritual realities, by the Holy Spirit, He *provided a complete furnishing, supplying and endowing of God's Kingdom truths and realities to them. Jesus supported them as He prepared them for their prophetic service to the Kingdom of God. He promoted and stimulated the exercise and growth of their "measure of faith", producing within them a mature "proportion of faith"*

What Jesus accomplished by demonstrating, instructing, training and mentoring His disciples when He was here, His "ascension gifts" are to conduct and accomplish with His followers around the world and in each generation, until Jesus returns at the end of this age. If we do not see the same results from the ascension gifts, today, that Jesus produced (and which the book of Acts describes and confirms), then we can contend that the focus and activities of the ascension gifts are missing their intended mark. The faith community and ascension gifts of Jesus, today, possess the same commission, equipping, Holy Spirit, authority and confirming witness of the Father that Jesus and the early Church believers possessed. If we aren't seeing these same spiritual activities and results, we must ask ourselves, "*Why?*".

Within the Church, today, we must re-establish our focus on the goals and responsibilities that Jesus and the Father gave us as Their covenant partners and representatives. God displayed His powerful, prophetic manifestations through His people in the Old Testament. He displayed His powerful, prophetic manifestations through Jesus and the early Church believers in the New Testament. There is no scriptural basis for us to even remotely question God's desire and intention to speak and act toward us in this same way, in our generation. *It is our over-dependence on our "natural", "soulish" orientation, combined with our general lack of knowledge, faith and experience in God's spiritual realities and prophetic manifestations, that is getting in our way.* Paul says to "*desire earnestly*"; to *covet* or *lust for* these prophetic manifestations of the Spirit.[111] If we don't covet them, we won't experience them. If we don't lust for them, we will end up like the 2½ tribes of Israel, who came up short of all that God had in store for them.

Extending & Expanding The Ministry of Jesus In Our Generation

In John chapter 1, Jesus, beginning His earthly ministry and making Himself known to the people who will become His disciples, saw Nathanael coming toward Him. Upon meeting him, Jesus shared information with Nathanael that was revealed to Him through the spiritual manifestation of a *word of knowledge*, by the Holy Spirit. This *word of knowledge* was communicated to Jesus by the Spirit, earlier, in a vision, where Jesus *saw* Nathanael under the fig tree. Being given this prophetic information by Jesus, Nathanael declared his belief that Jesus is the Messiah. Jesus responded, telling Nathanael that if he decides to follow Him, as His disciple, he will experience even more manifestations of the Spirit. John describes the introduction of Nathanael to Jesus, this way:

> *"Jesus saw Nathanael coming to Him, and said of him,* **"Behold, an Israelite indeed, in whom there is no deceit!"** *Nathanael said to Him, "How do You know me?" Jesus answered and said to him,* **"Before Philip called you, when you were under the fig tree, I saw you."** *Nathanael answered Him, "Rabbi, You are the Son of God; You are the King of Israel." Jesus answered and said to him, "Because I said to you that I saw you under the fig tree, do you believe?* **You will see greater things than**

---

[111] 1Corinthians 14:1

these." And He said to him, "Truly, truly, I say to you, you will see the heavens opened and the angels of God ascending and descending on the Son of Man."[112]

Jesus told Nathanael that he will see even greater prophetic manifestations than the particular *word of knowledge* He had just given him. Nathanael and the other disciples would see and experience angels engaged in Jesus' life and ministry, in order to minister to His needs and to participate and assist in the prophetic activities involved with Jesus' ministry.

We read these and other similar statements Jesus made and activities He conducted and assume that all of these things occurred in order to prove to His disciples that He is God. Yet, Jesus actually tells His disciples, and us, in these verses from John that these things would occur in His life *as the son of Man;* the son of Adam.

The Bible instructs us that angels are ministering spirits who are here to assist and serve the needs of God's covenant people.[113] Jesus wasn't the first person to have angels engaged in His life and ministry. We see angels at work in the lives of God's people in the Old Testament, as well as later, in the New Testament. Nathanael and others were astounded by the prophetic manifestations in Jesus' life and ministry because they had become almost completely naturally minded. They had lost all perspective of who they were, as *natural* and *spiritual* beings, and what they were created to be and do. This is the reason we read these scriptures and assume these things occurred in Jesus' life because He was God. *Jesus came as our visible, reliable example and to restore our perspective of who we are and what we are to accomplish, as God's image bearers and regents.*

Jesus lived His life and conducted His ministry on the earth as a human being, being led and empowered by the Holy Spirit. Many of these prophetic encounters, these *manifestations of the Spirit* that Jesus experienced and conducted within His ministry are similar to what God's people in the Old Testament experienced. They are the same prophetic manifestations and experiences that Paul lists in 1Corinthians 12-14, that we are all to experience and conduct in our

---

[112] John 1:47-51 NASB (emphasis mine)
[113] Hebrews 1:14; Acts 12:3-19; Acts 27:21-26; Psalm 91:11-12

lives and ministry activities under the New Covenant. *These people were amazed and often in disbelief at what Jesus said and did when He invited them to be His disciples. Yet, these are the very same people who experienced and conducted these same prophetic experiences and activities during the time they were being instructed, trained and mentored by Jesus for 3½ years, and after the Holy Spirit was poured out upon them on the Day of Pentecost.*

Jesus, as THE apostle, prophet, evangelist, pastor and teacher instructed, trained and mentored them in God's prophetic training. This training changed their frame of reference. It established a Kingdom perspective within their faith experience. It restored their orientation from a *natural* orientation to a *spiritual and natural* orientation. This Kingdom Discipleship training changed their *mode of operation*, just as it did with the children of Israel when God brought them out of Egypt and prophetically equipped and trained them for 40 years, preparing them to enter and possess their land of promise.

In our generation, as followers of Jesus, we have come to rely too much on our *natural, soulish* orientation and abilities, at the expense of our *spiritual* abilities. The words and spiritual activities of Jesus that we witness in the Bible profoundly amaze us. We assume they occurred because He was God. Our spiritual orientation has been ignored, dormant and uninstructed for so long that we don't realize these are the same spiritual manifestations we, ourselves, are to experience and conduct as God's earthly representatives. *This over-reliance on the natural and rational has robbed us of a dynamic, spiritual and faith-filled relationship with God, accompanied by these spiritual manifestations and prophetic encounters.*

We want our faith experience to be *easy, safe* and *predictable.* The life of faith, the faith of Abraham, is anything but that. Our individual and collective "measure of faith" is not being effectively exercised. We are not developing and producing the necessary regency relationship with God, our "proportion of faith", and the demonstration of the manifestations of the Spirit required to attain to "the measure of the stature which belongs to the fullness of Christ." *As the faith community of Jesus, we must honestly ask ourselves if we are truly "maturing in all aspects into Him who is the head, even Christ."*[114]

Will Our Current Proportion of Faith Be Enough?

In Luke 17 & 18, Jesus is instructing his disciples on events and activities that will occur on the earth at the time of His return. After identifying and describing some of these events, Jesus uses a parable to encourage His disciples to pray and never lose hope. At the end of this teaching, Jesus makes an amazing statement regarding God's desire and willingness to respond to the faith-filled prayers of His people:

> *"...now, **will not God bring about justice for His elect who cry to Him day and night, and will He delay long over them? I tell you that He will bring about justice for them quickly.** <u>**However**</u>, **when the Son of Man comes, will He find faith on the earth?**"* [115]

Jesus is instructing His disciples in the nature and character of the Father and His ability and willingness to respond to bring justice, quickly, in response to the faith-filled, enduring prayers of His covenant people. Yet, at the end of His teaching, Jesus begins His final statement with the word, *however*. Using *however*, Jesus makes a statement that seems to contrast or contradict the teaching He just gave them. God is able and willing to *quickly* respond to the faith-filled, enduring prayers of His people but the question Jesus asks is, *"Will He find His followers and representatives engaged in this enduring, faith-filled praying at the time when He returns?"* This is not a rhetorical question, but it is an open-ended question that is yet to be answered.

"The measure of faith" will be present at that time because there will be followers of Jesus on the earth when He returns. Yet, this is not the level of faith Jesus is asking about. He is asking if there will be an active, well-exercised and mature *proportion of faith* being utilized by God's covenant partners, in prayer, when He returns.

The answer to this question greatly depends on whether the ascension gifts are functioning, at that time, as Jesus intends and

---

[114] Ephesians 4:15
[115] Luke 18:7-8 NASB (emphasis mine)

commissioned them. If they are, then we will see the effective proclamation of the Kingdom of God taking place on the earth, by the followers of Jesus. We will see the demonstration of this reality with spiritual manifestations taking place through these covenant partners, by the Holy Spirit. We will see the Father confirming their testimony and this spiritual reality, with signs and wonders. But, if the ascension gifts aren't functioning as Jesus intends, then, most likely, we won't see them.

God has given humanity a mandate, a great commission, and He is not going to complete it for us. As a result, God works *in cooperation* with humanity to carry out His plans and purposes on Earth. *God's people must be actively and faithfully engaged with His Kingdom realities, events and activities.* God, in His sovereignty, has established it this way.

Today, do we see the followers of Jesus readily demonstrating and proclaiming the presence of the Kingdom of God on Earth, with manifestations of the Spirit taking place through their hands? Do we see God confirming their testimony and this prophetic reality, with signs and wonders? The answer is, generally, "No".

Therefore, we must conclude that the faith community of Jesus, right now, is not effectively executing the commission Jesus gave us in Mark 16:17-18. If true, then we must conclude that the ascension gifts of Jesus are not effectively executing the commission Jesus gave them in Ephesians 4.

This is an issue the entire Church must recognize. We must take action if we are to eventually complete our mandate. Incorrectly asserting that "God doesn't do these things anymore" or "God will sovereignly conduct these activities whether we are involved or not" only hinders our efforts.

The only way for Jesus' faith community to reverse this course is to acknowledge the reality of where we are, spiritually, and turn toward the biblical precedence God has established for the lives and ministries of His prophetic, covenant people. We must individually and as a faith community effectively exercise our proportion of faith and develop this enduring, faith-filled prayer that Jesus demonstrated and taught His disciples. We must believe and pray that God will reveal to us what we must do to return to the course

He established for us, from the beginning, and equipped and empowered us to travel. The question remains, "*Will Jesus find enduring, faith-filled covenant partners willing to engage and cooperate with Him in this way, before He returns?*

The Reward Of Faith-Filled Action

God, in His foreknowledge, gives us insight into the spiritual condition of His New Covenant people before Jesus returns. He gives us hope that we can and will turn this thing around; that we can effectively exercise and develop our proportion of faith, and engage in enduring, faith-filled prayer with God for this necessary change. God shows us that we will experience His ability and willingness to answer our prayers, quickly. He reveals to us that we will experience the ascension gifts of Jesus functioning as He intends. We will see the faith community of Jesus effectively proclaim and demonstrate the presence of the Kingdom of God, with signs and wonders confirming this reality:

> "*...this is what was spoken through the prophet Joel:* **'In the last days,** *God says,* **I will pour out my Spirit on all people.** *Your sons and daughters will prophesy. Your young will see visions. Your elders will dream dreams.* **Even upon my servants, men and women, I will pour out my Spirit in those days,** *and they will prophesy.* **I will cause wonders to occur in the heavens above and signs on the earth below, blood and fire and a cloud of smoke. The sun will be changed into darkness, and the moon will be changed into blood, before the great and spectacular day of the Lord comes.** *And everyone who calls on the name of the Lord will be saved.*'" [116]

Yes, this is the same prophecy from Joel that Peter declared was happening on the Day of Pentecost, in Acts 2, when the Holy Spirit was poured out upon the early Church believers. They proclaimed the presence of the Kingdom of God, made disciples of many nations, experienced and conducted prophetic manifestations by the

---

[116] Acts 2:16-21   CEB (emphasis mine)

Holy Spirit, and God confirmed their testimony and this Kingdom reality with signs and wonders.

Yet, the last part of this scripture from Joel 2 has yet to be fulfilled:

> *"I will cause wonders to occur in the heavens above and signs on the earth below, blood and fire and a cloud of smoke. The sun will be changed into darkness, and the moon will be changed into blood, before the great and spectacular day of the Lord comes. And everyone who calls on the name of the Lord will be saved."*

The fact is, the *Last Days* began on the Day of Pentecost and will continue until the return of Jesus to the earth. The *great and spectacular day of the Lord* speaks of the time of Jesus' return to establish the complete and visible Kingdom of God upon the earth. It is a time of tremendous chaos and upheaval, as well as tremendous displays of God's power and authority upon the earth, through His New Covenant people. *Even greater* prophetic spiritual realities and activities than what occurred in the early Church will occur *before the great and spectacular day of the Lord*. There is an *early* fulfillment of Joel's prophecy and a *latter* fulfillment. There was an *early rain* that initiated the birth and growth of the Church and there will be a *latter rain* that will bring the Church to its maturity, in preparation for the harvest and the return of Jesus.[117]

The Weeds Among The Wheat

There will be over 2000 years between the "sprouting" of Christianity on the Day of Pentecost and the "great harvest" into the Church before the return of Jesus. In the initial decades and centuries of the Church, we saw the followers of Jesus embrace and cooperate with God in proclamation and demonstration of the presence of the Kingdom of God throughout the known world. Though defeated by Jesus' death and resurrection, Satan and the domain of darkness remained active on the earth as a deceptive enemy against the generations of Jesus followers that were to follow.

---

[117] Joel 2:23-32; James 5:7

In an effort to minimize the growth and effectiveness of the Church and the Kingdom of God, Satan, using humans, introduced harmful heresies and other deceptive lies and practices into the Church's creed and experience. These "weeds" effectively spread, choking the life and spiritual experience of God's people. The Church's spiritual life with God and prophetic witness to the world slowly withered to a structured, regulated institution practicing formal religious observances, propagating oppressively harmful beliefs, and producing dead works. Though they spoke of themselves as the people of God, the Satanic heresies and evil culture of the world around them slowly corrupted their faith, bringing spiritual darkness – the Dark Ages.

These deceptive lies and heresies promoted by Satan and embraced by much of the faith community of God were many and varied. Some of these deceptive attacks are still found within the Church culture and experience, today. Here is a list of some of them:

- Salvation and restoration come through the attainment of divine knowledge and the expansion of the knowledge of one's self. The belief that the physical is evil and the spiritual is good (Gnosticism)

- Salvation is a combination of God's grace and an individual's efforts/deeds

- Jesus wasn't really human (Docetism); Jesus had only a divine nature (Monophysitism); Jesus did not have a human will (Monothelitism)

- Jesus wasn't God (Ebionism)

- Jesus had a human body and a divine mind (Apollinarianism)

- The institutional church acts as the mediator between God and the individual; the individual cannot relate directly with God

- The institutional church must interpret the scriptures for the individual; the individual cannot be trusted with the scriptures

- Salvation and its full benefit can only be experienced through the individual's loyal adherence to the orthodoxy and mediation of the institutional church

- Offering indulgences and other financial reparations to the institutional church will make the individual more worthy of God's favor

- God no longer conducts miracles, signs and wonders as He did in Bible times

- The Holy Spirit is not God; is not a living, active personality but is simply an impersonal force and influence for good in the world

God told us this deceptive effort by Satan, to corrupt the people of God and hinder the spread of the Kingdom of God, would happen. In Matthew's gospel, Jesus tells His disciples a parable to help explain what the Kingdom of God is like. In the parable, Jesus compares seed that is planted by the landowner with seed that is planted by his enemy, intended to ruin the landowner's crop and harvest:

> *"Jesus presented another parable to them, saying, "The kingdom of heaven may be compared to a man who sowed good seed in his field. But while his men were sleeping, **his enemy came and sowed tares among the wheat**, and went away. But **when the wheat sprouted and bore grain, then the tares became evident also**. The slaves of the landowner came and said to him, 'Sir, did you not sow good seed in your field? How then does it have tares?' And **he said to them, 'An enemy has done this!'** The slaves said to him, 'Do you want us, then, to go and gather them up?' But he said, 'No; for **while you are gathering up the tares, you may uproot the wheat with them. Allow both to grow together** until the harvest; and in the time of the harvest I will say to the reapers, "First gather up the tares and bind them in bundles to burn them up; but gather the wheat into my barn."""* [118]

This parable accurately describes what has taken place throughout Church history. The Kingdom of God was planted on the earth and into the lives of Jesus' disciples. Yet, in the midst of the initial growth of the Kingdom of God, "weeds" were also planted by "the enemy", Satan, in order to strangle and choke the growth of God's

---

[118] Matthew 13:24-30 NASB (emphasis mine)

Kingdom on earth and in future generations. As Jesus' parable articulates, God has allowed the "wheat" and the "weeds" to grow up together until the harvest, when the wheat will be separated from the weeds.

Learn From The Children of Israel

Will these weeds; these deceptive lies, heresies and practices from Satan keep the people of God and His Kingdom from accomplishing His plans for them? We can look at an example from the book of Exodus and see a parallel to this dynamic struggle. We see that God overcame the destructive effects of these "weeds" in the lives and experiences of the children of Israel, helping them to achieve what He had promised them.

Over the 400 years that the children of Israel were in Egypt, they increased in number to nearly a million people. During the entire 400 years, they considered themselves the people of God, even though they did not know Him and had not experienced His prophetic presence and activities within their faith experience.

Over time, as they became slaves to Pharaoh and the people of Egypt, they remembered God and called out to Him (prayed) for deliverance and freedom. God heard them and began His restoration process with them, delivering them from Egypt through His prophetic activities by the hand of Moses. God led them out of Egypt and toward the land He had promised them. They were God's covenant people, but they had been slowly and deceptively corrupted by the evil culture in Egypt, over those 400 years.

What did God do to restore them and His relationship with them, as their God? For 40 years He engaged them in His prophetic training activity, in the wilderness between Egypt and the land of promise. It was a deliberate restoration process filled with prophetic revelation, instruction, training and mentoring, both, individually and as a faith community. God had to let them see for themselves how deceptively corrupted they had become so they would willingly submit to Him and His training. The deception and evil culture of Egypt, which had slowly corrupted their souls (mind, emotions, will), had to be replaced with the truth and righteous culture of the Kingdom of God.

God's Restoration Process

As God led them, He did so by providing times of rest, after they had traveled for a period of time, moving forward toward the land of promise. It was during these times that God introduced Himself and His spiritual truths, realities and prophetic activities into their faith experience with Him. God was deliberately changing their kingdom orientation, over time. He gave the children of Israel seasons of rest so they could "process" what He was doing, and understand how to "come into agreement" with Him to implement and integrate these realities and activities into their individual and collective faith experience.

We can read about these times of prophetic encounter and revelation, and Israel's responses to these invitations from God to cooperate with Him. We often see their "carnal" reactions and imperfect efforts to process what they were experiencing. We see their struggles to effectively understand and grasp these realities in order to "come into agreement" with God concerning their implementation. They often battled with God and with each other in how to apply these realities and activities in meaningful and practical ways. They made mistakes as they worked to integrate them into their faith experience.

Kingdom re-orientation, and the spiritual nature of the truths, realities and prophetic activities associated with God and His Kingdom, is not an exact science. *It is a relational endeavor, with God and with each other.* We must enter into it and progress through it with faith, love, patience, humility, grace and forgiveness because each of us, all of us, will make mistakes, experience failures, and suffer setbacks as we travel on this journey to our land of promise. As God trains us in His spiritual, prophetic manifestations (*the gifts of the Spirit*), He uses our efforts and struggles to embrace and come into agreement with Him concerning their implementation, to develop His character qualities (*the fruit of the Spirit*) within us.

God introduced spiritual realities into their faith experience, using prophetic "invitations", and He gave them times of rest so they could embrace, process and understand how these realities impacted them, and how they should respond to them. This restoration process and prophetic training progressively prepared them to cooperate and work with God and with each other, as His co-laborers in His Kingdom activities.

This same restoration process and training is what God has been conducting within the Church over the centuries, since the Dark Ages. Even though the Church acknowledged that they were the people of God, the deceptive heresies and lies of Satan robbed them of their true prophetic relationship and experience with Him. Yet, God is never without a remnant; individuals who desire to seek Him faithfully and earnestly. This heretical slavery and institutional corruption drove God's faithful remnant of covenant followers to call out to the Lord (prayed) to be delivered from these lies and deceptions. God heard them and took it upon Himself to deliver them and put them on the path to achieve what He had promised them. He began the restoration process of His New Covenant people by engaging them in His prophetic Kingdom training and He has been engaging them in it, in every generation, ever since.

God Establishes A Communication & Training History With Us

God desires to establish a prophetic relationship and communication history with each of us and with His faith communities. Through these, the Holy Spirit is able to invite us to join Him in this restoration process. Recognizing and responding to His invitations is the first step toward Him revealing Himself, His spiritual realities, and His prophetic manifestations to us. We must respond to Him if we are to learn, grow and mature in our proportion of faith.

As with the children of Israel in the wilderness, the key to success with this restoration process and prophetic training is to experience, embrace, learn, implement, integrate and move forward. Each Kingdom truth and spiritual reality that God adds to our faith experience is to be integrated with those He has previously given to us. Each truth and reality does not "stand alone" and we should not consider and approach them in this way. All of them are to be embraced, learned and integrated together, within our faith experience, if they are to achieve their intended results in and through us.

God has been restoring these spiritual truths and prophetic realities to the Church, generation after generation, over the last several centuries. Each generation is to instruct, train and mentor the next generation so these realities can be integrated into the faith community's prophetic experience until we reach *"the time of the end"*. As with the children of Israel in the wilderness, God is training and preparing His New Covenant people to know Him and prophetically engage with Him in His divine activities, as they approach this "land of promise". God is restoring the Church so we are able to effectively and accurately proclaim the presence of the Kingdom of God, and prophetically demonstrate the reality of its presence, with God confirming this reality with signs and wonders. This must take place, as God intends, before Jesus returns.

We can see this deliberate, progressive restoration of the Church at work when we look back over the last few centuries and recent decades:

- The restoration of the Biblical truth that "the just shall live by faith" – the Protestant Reformation (1517 A.D. - Martin Luther)

- The restoration of the Word of God into the hands of the people – translation of the Bible from Latin into English (1525 A.D. - William Tyndale)

- The restoration of the "New Birth" – taught as a foundational Christian truth (1539 A.D. - Menno Simons)

- The restoration of Personal Holiness (1700s - John Wesley and others)

- The restoration of the modern Missionary movement (1800s - William Carey and others)

- The restoration of the power of personal prayer (1800s - E.M. Bounds and others)

- The restoration of the presence and power of the Holy Spirit (early 1900s - the Azusa Street Revival and others)

- The restoration of the miracle working power of the Holy Spirit (1940s - Oral Roberts, Kathryn Kuhlman, William Branham, T. L. Osborn, and others)

- The restoration of personal and mass Evangelism (1950s - Billy Graham and others)
- The restoration of the manifestations of the Holy Spirit (1960s-1970s - the Jesus Movement/Charismatic Movement)
- The restoration of corporate praise and worship (1970s-1980s - Global Worship movement)
- The restoration of the prophetic activities of the Kingdom of God and the ministry of the Prophet (1980s-1990s - the global Prophetic movement)
- The restoration of global prophetic prayer (2000s-2010s - Global Prayer movement; Houses of Prayer)

The Generational Elders

God continues to restore and train us as we respond to His invitations and integrate His truths and realities into our faith experience with Him, generation after generation. As with the children of Israel, God has established what I call *generational elders* who experience and integrate these restored realities into their personal faith experience, as well as the experience of the faith community within their generation. These generational elders instruct, train and mentor the generations that follow them in these integrated realities, as well as provide wisdom and guidance in regard to the new restorative truths and activities God introduces and engages in with us.

In our day, a generation of elders has grown up with and experienced the restoration of *personal and mass evangelism, the miracle working power of the Holy Spirit, the manifestations and operations of the Holy Spirit, prophetic praise and worship, the prophetic activities of the Kingdom of God, and night and day prophetic prayer as the House of Prayer for all nations.* They have recognized these activities as being from God, have embraced them, and have learned to "come into agreement with God" for how He wants us to implement them within the life of the individual believer and the entire faith community. They have integrated these Kingdom realities and prophetic activities with those God has previously restored to the Church.

The purpose of all of this is for each generation to train and mentor those who follow, so each generation can progress beyond the understanding and prophetic realities experienced by the previous generations. This is why the ascension gifts of Jesus must recapture their original mission and be restored to what Jesus intended when He gave them to the Church. *They must work in cooperation with the generational elders and the prophetic ministry and activities of the Holy Spirit. This is all part of God's Kingdom Discipleship process.* This "coming alongside" of the next generation is a critical component of God's restoration and training.

As the prophetic scriptures tell us, these critical restorative activities will occur. The Church will respond to the invitations and activities of God in these final days. The people of God will engage in the enduring, faith-filled prayer necessary to turn our present condition around. God will hear and willingly answer our prayers, quickly. The ascension gifts, generational elders and faith community of Jesus will come into agreement with God's plans and established destiny. The apostle, prophet, evangelist, pastor and teacher will return to the correct course and engage in the prophetic instructing, training and mentoring activities necessary to prepare the Church for their service to the Kingdom of God. The Church will exercise and develop their *measure of faith*, so as to employ their *proportion of faith* in the manifestations of the Spirit, as witnesses to the presence of the Kingdom of God. God will confirm their testimony and this reality with signs and wonders that the world has never seen before. As a result, *"all who call on the name of the Lord will be saved"*.

The question is, who among us will choose to respond to God's invitations and participate with Him in these spiritual activities? Who will *"deny himself, take up his cross and follow"* Jesus, as He did for the Father when He was here? Who will pass the "tests" that determine who is courageous, prepared and spiritually disciplined enough to engage in the prophetic battles necessary to enter and possess our "land of promise"?

Learn From The Examples God Gave Us

When Joshua and the children of Israel were preparing to enter the Promised Land, God spoke to Joshua and told him to *"only be strong and very courageous"*.[119] When God spoke to Gideon and instructed him to test the people who were with him, He told Gideon that those who were fearful and those who were not trained and prepared, should go home because they were not able to effectively engage and cooperate with God in the prophetic battle that was to come. Of the 32,000 who began with Gideon, only 300 were courageous and prepared enough, according to God's criteria, to engage in the coming battle. These 300 were required to obediently respond to all that God prophetically instructed them to do, which was to, essentially, break some clay pots and scream at the enemy. They had to trust God that their obedience to His instructions, which seemed completely irrational and impossible, would be sufficient to win this battle. This was to be a prophetic battle and it was to be God's battle. They simply had to be courageous, effectively trained and disciplined, and prepared to respond with obedience to whatever God told them to do.[120] This spiritual, prophetic training and preparation doesn't happen overnight.

The Bible tells us that God is not bound to save or deliver by many or by few.[121] He doesn't need any of us. Yet, He chooses to engage with us because He gave the earth and its governance to humanity, and He will engage with human beings to take action in the affairs of earth. The important point of this is, *God will engage with humanity in the affairs of earth but humanity must engage and participate with God on His terms, according to His plans and strategies, being trained and prepared according to His established criteria, not our own.* God's activities on the earth are prophetic activities. If we are going to participate with Him in these activities, we must prepare to respond to and participate with Him, prophetically.

God has been restoring and preparing the Church for the great battle that it is coming at the end of the age. It will be a prophetic battle and we must be prepared and trained to engage in the battle, and the events leading up to it. We must be able to listen and hear His instructions for us and respond with obedience, courage and

---

[119] Joshua 1:6-9

[120] Judges 7

[121] 1Samuel 14:6

faith. We are all *enrolled* in His prophetic training but are we actively *engaged* in it? God is on a mission and He has a timetable for completing our training. We are nearing, if not already engaged in the early stages of *the time of the end*. All that we have been discussing and describing will take place *before the great and spectacular day of the Lord comes*. We must take the next step, now, toward this prophetic fulfillment. We must "turn around" and get back on the correct course that God has prepared for us. God is inviting us and He's waiting for us to respond.

Yet, realize this: *The return of Jesus at the end of the age does not complete humanity's mandate. There is more to accomplish!*

- *Takeaways for the reader*:

  o Through the New Birth, the *"circumcision of the heart"*, we are covenant partners with God and recipients and beneficiaries of His covenant promises

  o We are to proclaim the presence of the Kingdom of God on the earth, and visually demonstrate the reality of its presence, as witnesses, with manifestations of the Holy Spirit

  o We are engaged in God's restoration process and prophetic training, where He reveals, instructs, trains and mentors us, by the Holy Spirit, in who He is and in His Kingdom realities and prophetic activities

  o The correct functioning of the ascension gifts of Jesus and the manifestations and operations of the Holy Spirit are critical to the growth and maturing of the faith community of Jesus before His return

  o We must exercise and develop our *measure of faith* so we can effectively engage the *proportion of our faith* in the prophetic activities of the Kingdom of God, as we move closer to *the time of the end*

- *Small group questions*:

  - Jesus gave the Apostle, Prophet, Evangelist, Pastor and Teacher to us to equip us for service to the Kingdom of God, and to support us as we grow and mature in God's prophetic training.

    - What does that mean?

    - What is the role of the Apostle in the faith community of God? How has the Apostle's ministry equipped and supported you in your faith experience with God?

    - What is the role of the Prophet in the faith community of God? How has the Prophet's ministry equipped and supported you in your faith experience with God?

    - What is the role of the Evangelist in the faith community of God? How has the Evangelist's ministry equipped and supported you in your faith experience with God?

    - Can we be effectively and successfully prepared and trained if these three vital ministries are not actively and correctly functioning within Gods' faith community, as Jesus established them?

  - When we are born again and restored to our relationship with God and our role and function within the Kingdom of God, we are given *the measure of faith*. As we respond to God's invitations to engage with Him in His prophetic training, we exercise that measure of faith to develop and increase our *proportion of faith*.

    - How does exercising our *measure* of faith in our relationship with God and in the gifts and manifestations of the Spirit increase the *proportion* of our faith?

- Why does God tell us to *earnestly desire* the manifestations of the Spirit?

- How do these manifestations of the Spirit operate prophetically in and through our lives? What are they to accomplish?

☐ If you are enrolled in God's prophetic training, and are to be prepared to engage in God's prophetic Kingdom activities and battles, moving forward, how would you evaluate your progress?

- Are you prepared to hear God's specific prophetic instructions when they are directly given to you?

- Are you prepared to respond obediently to them, in confident faith, regardless of how impossible and irrational they may seem to you?

- Are you prepared to directly and prophetically confront and engage the powers of darkness, and their human representatives, with courage and confidence, when the situation arises?

- On a scale of 1 – 10, with 1 being *completely unprepared* and 10 being *ready to engage in all of these things, today,* where do you consider yourself on this scale, and why? If you have more progress to make, what would be your *next steps*?

CHAPTER 7

BUT THE PEOPLE WHO KNOW THEIR GOD

*"And armed forces of his shall appear [in the holy land] and they shall pollute the sanctuary, the [spiritual] stronghold, and shall take away the continual [daily burnt offering]; and **they shall set up [in the sanctuary] the abomination that astonishes and makes desolate** [probably an altar to a pagan god]. And such as violate the covenant he shall pervert and seduce with flatteries, **but the people who know their God shall prove themselves strong and shall stand firm and do exploits [for God]."** And **they who are wise and understanding among the people shall instruct many and make them understand**, though some [of them and their followers] shall fall by the sword and flame, by captivity and plunder, for many days. Now when they fall, they shall receive a little help. Many shall join themselves to them with flatteries and hypocrisies. And **some of those who are wise, prudent, and understanding shall be weakened and fall, [thus, then, the insincere among the people will lose courage and become deserters. It will be a test] to refine, to purify, and to make those among [God's people] white, even to the time of the end**, because it is yet for the time [God] appointed."* Daniel 11:31-35 – Amplified Classic Bible (emphasis mine)

*"Now at that time Michael, the great prince who stands guard over the sons of your people, will arise. And **there will be a time of distress such as never occurred since there was a nation until that time**; and at that time your people, everyone who is found written in the book, will be rescued. Many of those who sleep in the dust of the ground will awake, these to everlasting life, but the others to disgrace and everlasting contempt. **Those who have insight will shine brightly like the brightness of the expanse of heaven, and those who lead the many to righteousness, like the stars forever and ever**. But as for you, Daniel, **conceal these words and seal up the book until***

the end of time; many will go back and forth, and knowledge will increase." Daniel 12:1-4 NASB (emphasis mime)

God has told us from the beginning that humanity will complete their mandate, that Satan and the powers of darkness will be defeated, and what will happen at *the time of the end.* God has spoken to us at various times and through various individuals, throughout human history, so we will not be uninformed of what is to come and be without understanding and unprepared when it arrives. One such person through whom God spoke and gave us a tremendous amount of information regarding these end-time events and activities was the prophet Daniel.

Daniel was an Old Testament prophet as well as a high-ranking government official who served several heathen kings during his lifetime. He lived in the 6th century B.C.. When the armies of king Nebuchadnezzar defeated Judah and captured the city of Jerusalem, Daniel was one of a group of young Hebrew men who were taken captive to Babylon, in 605 B.C., to serve in the court of Nebuchadnezzar. Babylon was located in what is now the country of Iraq.

Daniel was held in high esteem by Nebuchadnezzar and placed in a high government position as a result of having correctly interpreted the king's troubling dream. Even though Babylon was later overthrown by the Medes and Persians, and they set several kings upon the throne in Babylon, Daniel continued to serve in the court of these kings throughout his lifetime. During his lengthy life and service in Babylon, Daniel faithfully served God and experienced many prophetic dreams, visions and angelic visitations.

Most of these prophetic visions were centered on events involving God's people in the future, most notably during what we call *the time of the end.* Several of these prophecies were to have a dual fulfillment. By *dual fulfillment,* I mean that the prophecy was to have a "lesser" or more narrow scope in regard to its initial fulfillment, usually involving the Jewish people at some point in their collective experience. Yet, the prophecy was also intended to have a "greater" or expanded scope in its final fulfillment, on a grander scale, usually involving all of humanity and relating to *the time of the end.*

Examples of a dual fulfillment prophecy are some of the prophecies concerning the coming of the Messiah. These prophecies have a "lesser" scope when they are initially fulfilled at Jesus' first coming to the earth as the *suffering servant*, and His activities are focused, predominantly, on the Jewish people and the area we know as *the holy land*. Yet, they will have a "greater" fulfillment at Jesus' second coming as the *conquering King*, and His activities will be expanded to include all of humanity and the entire earth.

We saw another dual fulfillment prophecy, earlier in the book, from Joel chapter 2, where the Holy Spirit was poured out on the early followers of Jesus, on the Day of Pentecost, in Acts chapter 2[122] This was the early fulfillment; the *early rain* intended to enable and empower the initial sprouting and growth of the Church. Yet, we also see that there will be a second fulfillment of Joel's prophecy; the outpouring of the Holy Spirit or *latter rain*, that will enable and empower the final harvest of people, from across the entire earth, coming into the Kingdom of God before *the time of the end* and Jesus' return to rule the earth.[123]

The future events that Daniel saw and prophesied, and the specifics of what will occur, give us tremendous insight into the nature and foreknowledge of God and His ability to know the end from the beginning, as it relates to humanity. Nothing is hidden from His sight. In eternity, God has already seen what will occur, in time, before it ever happens. Some of what God has already planned and seen He revealed to Daniel through these prophetic dreams, visions and angelic visitations. God is a communicator and a revealer of mysteries.[124] He wants us to know who He is, what He is doing, and what He will do, in its time, as it relates to His restoration process for humanity.

Through these divine, prophetic revelations, we are able to see the continued rise and influence of Satan and evil upon the Jewish people, and all of humanity, as well as the events that God uses to encounter and engage humanity in order to restore us. This dramatic rise and increase of Satan, as well as the dramatic rise and

---

[122] Joel 2:23

[123] James 5:7

[124] Daniel 2:47

increase of God's restorative activities in and through His people, provides the backdrop for a definitive prophetic, spiritual battle that will be fought within a war that has already been won. It will be a conflict that is the beginning of the end for Satan. This conflict will commence the prophetic activities of God that will usher in the complete and utter demise and dismantling of Satan and his domain of darkness. Jesus won the war with His death and resurrection. God's New Covenant people will begin the systematic dismantling of Satan's evil and rebellious operation, with Jesus as their King and Leader, as they move forward to complete humanity's divine mandate.

God began telling us of this great, end-time conflict early in human history. We don't have a record of the specific event where God revealed this information, but we do have a record of what He revealed. It is in the book of Jude:

> "It was also about these men that **Enoch, in the seventh generation from Adam, prophesied**, saying, "Behold, the Lord came with many thousands of His holy ones, to execute judgment upon all, and to convict all the ungodly of all their ungodly deeds which they have done in an ungodly way, and of all the harsh things which ungodly sinners have spoken against Him." [125]

God revealed to Enoch, one of the early descendants of Adam; a man who *"walked with God; and he was not, for God took him"*[126], what was to take place thousands of years in the future, at *the time of the end* and the return of Jesus to rule the earth. God cryptically told humanity, then, that we would eventually complete our divine mandate.

God also revealed to the apostle John, near the end of his life, many things that will take place at *the time of the end*, in the book of Revelation. Throughout human history, God has revealed these end time events and activities so we can know what is to occur and how we are to participate with Him in these events.

---

[125] Jude 14-15 NASB (emphasis mine)
[126] Genesis 5:24

God reveals to us a great deal of information concerning the natural and spiritual environments and activities occurring in the period of time leading up to *the time of the end*. When Jesus was asked by His disciples what it will be like at the end of the age, Jesus responded by saying:

> **"See to it that no one misleads you**. *For many will come in My name, saying, 'I am the Christ,' and will mislead many. You will be hearing of wars and rumors of wars.* **See that you are not frightened, for those things must take place, but that is not yet the end.** *For nation will rise against nation, and kingdom against kingdom, and in various places there will be famines and earthquakes.* **But all these things are merely the beginning of birth pangs.** *Then* **they will deliver you to tribulation, and will kill you, and you will be hated by all nations because of My name. At that time many will fall away and will betray one another and hate one another.** *Many false prophets will arise and will mislead many.* **Because lawlessness is increased, most people's love will grow cold.** *But the one who endures to the end, he will be saved.* **This gospel of the kingdom shall be preached in the whole world as a testimony to all the nations, and then the end will come."** [127]

In Matthew 24, Jesus gives us a great deal of information regarding attitudes, events and activities as they relate to people and the earth, in the time leading up to His return:

- See to it that no one misleads you
- Many will come saying they are the Messiah, and will mislead many
- See that you are not frightened
- You will hear of wars and rumors of wars but that is not yet the end
- Nation will rise against nation, and kingdom against kingdom
- In various places there will be famines and earthquakes

---

[127] Matthew 24:4-14 NASB (emphasis mine)

- They will deliver you to tribulation, and will kill you, and you will be hated by all nations because of being a Jesus follower
- Many will fall away and will betray one another and hate one another
- Many false prophets will arise and will mislead many
- Because lawlessness is increased, most people's love will grow cold
- The one who endures to the end will be saved
- The gospel of the Kingdom of God shall be preached in the whole world as a witness to all the nations, and then the end will come

We have seen and will continue to see these attitudes, events and activities in our world, and they will only increase in frequency and magnitude. Jesus, in His rebuke of the Pharisees when they asked Him for a sign from heaven to prove that He is the Messiah, said to them:

"When it is evening, you say, 'It will be fair weather, for the sky is red'. And in the morning, 'There will be a storm today, for the sky is red and threatening.' Do you know how to discern the appearance of the sky, but cannot discern the signs of the times?" [128]

Jesus wants us to know what is going to happen, not only at the time of His return but in the period leading up to it. He wants us to discern the signs of the times, and He has given us clear information of what those times will look like and how we can prepare for them. Today, there is much being seen and discussed regarding the weather changes, climate changes, geological changes, geo-political changes, and even the changes in how Christianity is expressed and perceived. Human love and compassion is growing cold due to the lawlessness occurring all around us. Violence and hatred are running rampant throughout the world. As Jesus said, these are only the birth pangs; the beginning of the birthing process that will bring about His return.

Yet, there is a "sign of the times" that has yet to be witnessed in the manner that Jesus said would take place before His return. It is *"the*

---

[128] Matthew 16:2-4 NASB (emphasis mine)

latter rain" that Joel prophesied about; the *manner* and *magnitude* in which the message of the Kingdom of God is to be communicated and demonstrated to the entire world, by God's covenant people. In Matthew 24: 14, Jesus tells us:

> *"This gospel of the kingdom shall be preached in the whole world **as a testimony** (witness) **to all the nations**, and then the end will come."*

In an earlier chapter we saw what this word *testimony* or *witness* means; that it requires a personal experience of an event or activity, along with the ability to testify to and demonstrate that first-hand experience. This is what Jesus means when He says that *the gospel of the kingdom of God shall be preached to the whole world as a testimony to all the nations*. It will be a *vocal* and *demonstrated* testimony and witness to the entire world.

The Gates Of Hell Shall Not Prevail Against It

Jesus had something to say to His disciples concerning the purpose, nature and activities of His followers, the Church, once He ascended back to the Father. One day, as He was instructing them in the realities and activities of the Kingdom of God, Jesus turned to His disciples and asked them, *"Who do people say that I am?"* Simon responded that He is the Messiah, the Son of God. Responding to Simon, Jesus declares several very important spiritual realities that the followers of Jesus must recognize, understand and come into agreement with God, concerning their fulfillment. Jesus responded to Simon, saying:

> *"Blessed (happy, fortunate, and to be envied) are you, Simon Bar-Jonah. For flesh and blood [men] have not revealed this to you, but My Father Who is in heaven. And I tell you, you are Peter [Greek, Petros—a large piece of rock], and on this rock [Greek, petra—a huge rock like Gibraltar] I will build My church, and **the gates of Hades (the powers of the infernal region) shall not overpower it [or be strong to its detriment or hold out against it]**. I will give you the keys of the kingdom of heaven; and **whatever you bind (declare to be improper and unlawful) on earth <u>must be what is</u>***

already bound in heaven; and whatever you loose (declare lawful) on earth must be what is already loosed in heaven. [129]

In response to Simon's confession, Jesus made this prophetic declaration:

- God the Father revealed to Simon that Jesus is the Messiah
- As a result, Simon's name will now be Peter
- Upon the truth of Peter's revelation and confession, Jesus' faith community will be built
- Satan and the domain of darkness will be defeated and not be able to over-power or stand against the mission and activities of the Kingdom of God and His faith community
- Jesus will give His followers the authority of the Kingdom of God to use on the earth, on His behalf
- What Jesus and the Father, in heaven, determine and authorize, Their faith community, on the earth, will accomplish as Their representatives and regents.

Jesus is telling His disciples that He is restoring humanity to their created place and function as God's representatives and regents on the earth. They will possess the Kingdom authority, ability and tools to carry out the prophetic activities the Father and Jesus, in heaven, communicate to them to accomplish, on Their behalf. *Satan and the domain of darkness will be defeated and will not be able to overpower or stand against the authority and ability Jesus' followers will possess and exercise to accomplish these divinely authorized Kingdom activities.* Humanity will complete their divine mandate, including the condition to subdue the earth, and Satan won't be able to stop it.

This is the purpose of God's restoration process and His prophetic training; to reveal, instruct, train and mentor Jesus' followers in these spiritual realities and prophetic activities so we can faithfully complete what He commissions us to accomplish. This is why the ascension gifts must function as Jesus intended, and why the generational elders must come along side of the younger followers of

---

[129] Matthew 16:17-19 Amplified Classic Bible

Jesus, to instruct, train and mentor them in these realities and activities. Both groups are crucial to the spiritual and prophetic development and equipping of the Church, in every generation, as we approach *the time of the end.*

To bring context to the importance of this restoration process and prophetic training, moving forward, let's take a look at some of what God tells us will happen as we approach and enter into *the time of the end.*

The Antichrist & The Abomination of Desolation

To open this chapter, I quoted two scriptures from the book of Daniel, which were taken from one of Daniel's prophetic experiences; being visited by an angel. In this experience, the angel gave Daniel an event by event synopsis of what was to take place in the future, regarding the people of God, including major events taking place at *the time of the end.* In the first prophetic scripture from Daniel, the angel tells him:

*"And armed forces of his shall appear [in the holy land] and they shall pollute the sanctuary, the [spiritual] stronghold, and shall take away the continual [daily burnt offering]; and **they shall set up [in the sanctuary] the abomination that astonishes and makes desolate** [probably an altar to a pagan god]. And such as violate the covenant he shall pervert and seduce with flatteries, **but the people who know their God shall prove themselves strong and shall stand firm and do exploits [for God]."** And **they who are wise and understanding among the people shall instruct many and make them understand,** though some [of them and their followers] shall fall by the sword and flame, by captivity and plunder, for many days. Now when they fall, they shall receive a little help. Many shall join themselves to them with flatteries and hypocrisies. And **some of those who are wise, prudent, and understanding shall be weakened and fall, [thus, then, the insincere among the people will lose courage and become deserters. It will be a test] to refine, to purify, and to make those among [God's***

people] white, even to the time of the end, because it
is yet for the time [God] appointed." [130]

The angel tells Daniel several things that are very important to us,
beginning with the rise of a king who will act wickedly against the
people of God, as no person before him. He will exalt himself and
stand, defiantly, in the face of God.

Earlier in this chapter I mentioned that there are prophetic
scriptures that will have a dual fulfillment, and I gave some
examples. This prophecy in Daniel is a prophetic scripture that has
a dual fulfillment. The initial, "lesser" fulfillment refers to an event
that took place in the second century, B.C.. Antiochus Epiphanes, a
heathen king who hated the Jewish people, plundered Jerusalem,
installing the likeness of Zeus within the Jewish temple.

This initial invasive and destructive activity of Antiochus Epiphanes
upon the Jewish people, and the installation of the original
"abomination of desolation" within the Jewish temple, was only a
foreshadowing of the ultimate fulfillment of the prophecy. This final
fulfillment will be the invasion of the Jewish homeland and the
installation of the paramount "abomination of desolation" within
the Jewish temple that will take place at *the time of the end*, by the
Antichrist, himself.

Jesus, speaking to His disciples, refers to this same scripture in
Daniel 11, nearly 200 years *after* the invasion by Antiochus
Epiphanes, to describe the second, final fulfillment of the
"abomination of desolation" that will take place in the future, shortly
before His return to the earth:

> *"Therefore **when you see the ABOMINATION OF
> DESOLATION which was spoken of through Daniel
> the prophet, standing in the holy place** (let the reader
> understand), then those who are in Judea must flee to the
> mountains. Whoever is on the housetop must not go down
> to get the things out that are in his house. Whoever is in the
> field must not turn back to get his cloak. But woe to those
> who are pregnant and to those who are nursing babies in
> those days! But pray that your flight will not be in the*

---

[130] Daniel 11:31-35 – Amplified Classic Bible (emphasis mine)

*winter, or on a Sabbath. **For then there will be a great tribulation, such as has not occurred since the beginning of the world until now, <u>nor ever will</u>. Unless those days had been cut short, no life would have been saved; <u>but for the sake of the elect those days will be cut short</u>.**"* [131]

Jesus quotes Daniel 11, stating that this "abomination of desolation" event has not yet been completely fulfilled. Even though Antiochus Epiphanes fulfilled the scripture in Daniel to a lesser extent, the complete, ultimate fulfillment will not take place until *the time of the end.*

This end-time king, the Antichrist, will carry out an unprecedented assault against God, the Jewish people in Jerusalem, and the "elect"; the followers of Jesus living on the earth. The Antichrist will initiate this assault by directly attacking Jerusalem and the revered place of worship, the Jewish temple. He will invade the Holy Land and setup an image of himself within the Jewish temple, establishing the paramount "abomination of desolation" that Jesus is referring to. Jesus says that this event will initiate what He describes as, "*a great tribulation, such as has not occurred since the beginning of the world until now, nor ever will. Unless those days had been cut short, no life would have been saved; <u>but for the sake of the elect those days will be cut short</u>.*"

Why must these events be cut short, by God, for the sake of the followers of Jesus? Humanity cannot complete our divine mandate if all life on earth is destroyed. There will be no one left to fill the earth. There will be nothing and no one to rule and govern. Those on the earth who must be subdued will not be left alive to subdue. With all life on earth destroyed, humanity cannot complete our divine mandate. For the sake of redeemed humanity and the completion of our mandate, all life on earth will not be destroyed. Satan will not be able to carry out his plan to do so.

Humanity's Sin & Rebellion Against God Will Reach Its Full Measure

---

[131] Matthew 24:15-22 NASB (emphasis mine)

Paul describes the activities of the Antichrist this way, in his second letter to the church at Thessalonica, when he instructs them concerning the events that will occur leading up to the return of Jesus:

> *"Let no one in any way deceive you, for it will not come **unless the apostasy comes first**, and **the man of lawlessness is revealed, the son of destruction, who opposes and exalts himself above every so-called god or object of worship, so that he takes his seat in the temple of God, displaying himself as being God.** Do you not remember that while I was still with you, I was telling you these things? And you know what restrains him now, so that in his time he will be revealed. For the mystery of lawlessness is already at work; only he who now restrains will do so until he is taken out of the way. **Then that lawless one will be revealed whom the Lord will slay with the breath of His mouth and bring to an end by the appearance of His coming; that is, the one whose coming is in accord with the activity of Satan, with all power and signs and false wonders, and with all the deception of wickedness** for those who perish, **because they did not receive the love of the truth so as to be saved."** [132]*

Jesus, as well as Paul, Peter and other Biblical writers tell us that the people of God will come under tremendous persecution in the days leading up to the return of Jesus. As the tremendous *latter rain* prophetic activities of the Kingdom of God are occurring through the hands of God's people, as a witness to the reality and presence of the Kingdom on the earth, great persecution against them will also occur. Many will suffer martyrdom[133] at the hands of the kings of the earth. These followers of Jesus will stand against the demonic influence and activities of Satan and the Antichrist, *for a time.* I say *for a time* because there will come a time when God allows the Antichrist and the kings of the earth to temporarily overcome the people of God, shortly before the return of Jesus. Why will God do this? Because He will allow humanity's sin, rebellion and evil to

---

[132] 2Thessalonians 2:3-20 NASB (emphasis mine)
[133] Revelation 7:9-17

reach its maturity, its full measure, before His wrath is poured out upon them:

> *"It was also given to him to make war with the saints and to overcome them, and authority over every tribe and people and tongue and nation was given to him."* [134]

The revealing of the Antichrist and his assault upon God, the followers of Jesus, Jerusalem, the Jewish people and their temple, and the entire world is an important event for us to be knowledgeable about as we move forward toward the time of Jesus' return to the earth.

The Great Falling Away

In regard to many within the faith community of Jesus at that time, the angel goes on to tell Daniel:

> *"Many shall join themselves to them with flatteries and hypocrisies. And some of those who are wise, prudent, and understanding shall be weakened and fall,* **[thus, then, the insincere among the people will lose courage and become deserters.** *It will be a test] to refine, to purify, and to make those among [God's people] white, even to the time of the end, because it is yet for the time [God] appointed."*

This portion of Daniel's prophecy describes the apostasy, "the great falling away" from the faith that Jesus, Paul, Peter, the writer of *Hebrews,* and others tell us will take place at *the time of the end.* They tell us that a Satanic attack will come against the Church, both, from the outside and from within. *"Many shall join themselves to them with flatteries and hypocrisies."* The people of God will be tested through this attack, this infiltration of "false brethren" into the Church. These false brethren will endeavor to turn the people of God against Him and against each other, their leaders, and those who are engaged in the spiritual battle at hand. But as Jesus told us:

---

[134] Revelation 13:7 NASB

"Then they will deliver you to tribulation, and will kill you, and you will be hated by all nations because of My name. **At that time many will fall away and will betray one another and hate one another. Many false prophets will arise and will mislead many. Because lawlessness is increased, most people's love will grow cold.** *But the one who endures to the end, he will be saved."* [135]

As much as the followers of Jesus will experience the dynamic prophetic activities of the Kingdom of God in the time leading up to the return of Jesus, there will be many who will turn from God through deception, insincerity, and their inability to maintain a heart of love and compassion in the midst of the unprecedented lawlessness and evil occurring around them. The Church will be attacked from within, on several fronts.

Paul, in his second letter to Timothy, his child in the faith, describes the attitudes and activities that people will have and engage in, at this time:

"But realize this, that in the last days difficult times will come. For men will be lovers of self, lovers of money, boastful, arrogant, revilers, disobedient to parents, ungrateful, unholy, unloving, irreconcilable, malicious gossips, without self-control, brutal, haters of good, treacherous, reckless, conceited, lovers of pleasure rather than lovers of God, **holding to a form of godliness, although they have denied its power;** *avoid such men as these."* [136]

If we look at what Paul is telling us, here, and look at the context in which he is saying it, we will recognize something that should make all of us sit up and take notice. In chapters 2 and 3 of his second letter to Timothy, Paul is instructing Timothy concerning his responsibilities within the community of believers, the Church. Paul tells us that the ungodly attitudes and activities that will occur in the world, in the last days, will deceptively find their way into Jesus' faith communities. Paul tells us that these ungodly attitudes and

---

[135] Matthew 24:9-13 NASB (emphasis mine)
[136] 2Timothy 3:1-5 NASB (emphasis mine)

activities will be introduced into our churches and gatherings by those who Paul identifies as *"evil men and impostors"*.[137]

Paul warns us that:

> *"Now **in a large house there are not only gold and silver vessels, but also vessels of wood and of earthenware, and some to honor and some to dishonor.** Therefore, **if anyone cleanses himself from these things, he will be a vessel for honor**, sanctified, useful to the Master, prepared for every good work."* [138]

In our churches and gatherings, there are those who seek to cause disturbances and divisions among us, as they prey upon the immature and those weighed down with sin and struggles.[139] Paul calls these infiltrators *"evil men and impostors who will proceed from bad to worse, **deceiving and being deceived.**"*[140] Paul exposes them to us by telling us that they will be, *"...**holding to a form of godliness, although they have denied its power**; avoid such men as these."* [141] He goes on to tell us that, *"...**these men also oppose the truth**, men of depraved mind, **rejected in regard to the faith. But they will not make further progress**; for their folly will be obvious to all"*[142]

Paul is describing individuals who, at one time, may have pursued faith in Christ. Yet, they allowed the evil, destructive attitudes and deceptive lies of the enemy, which run rampant and are perpetrated upon those who are in the world, to deceive them. *These deceptions develop into a religious philosophy and practice that espouses a false "godliness" and denies the true gospel of Jesus Christ and the power of God that is resident within it.* These individuals will prey upon the Church in the last days, as never before.

Jude, in his letter, also warns us of this end-time assault upon the Church, when he writes:

---

[137] 2Timothy 3:13

[138] 2Timothy 2:20-21 NASB

[139] 2Timothy 3:6-7

[140] 2Timothy 3:13 NASB (emphasis mine)

[141] 2Timothy 3:5 NASB (emphasis mine)

[142] 2Timothy 3:8-9 NASB (emphasis mine)

*"For certain persons have crept in unnoticed, those who were long beforehand marked out for this condemnation, **ungodly persons who turn the grace of our God into licentiousness and deny our only Master and Lord, Jesus Christ**...these men, also by dreaming, **defile the flesh, and reject authority, and revile angelic majesties. But these men revile the things which they do not understand**; and the things which they know by instinct, like unreasoning animals, by these things they are destroyed. Woe to them! **These are the men who are hidden reefs in your love feasts when they feast with you without fear**, caring for themselves; **clouds without water, carried along by winds; autumn trees without fruit, doubly dead, uprooted; wild waves of the sea, casting up their own shame like foam; wandering stars**, for whom the black darkness has been reserved forever. **These are grumblers, finding fault, following after their own lusts; they speak arrogantly, flattering people for the sake of gaining an advantage. "In the last time there will be mockers, following after their own ungodly lusts." These are the ones who cause divisions, worldly-minded, devoid of the Spirit."* [143]

In the last days there will be an unprecedented Satanic attack upon the Church from those who are deceived and have come into our churches, gatherings and "love feasts" in order to deceive, if possible, even those who are sincere followers of Jesus. Paul continues with this end-times warning for the Church, when He says:

*"But the Spirit explicitly says that **in later times some will fall away from the faith, paying attention to deceitful spirits and doctrines of demons, by means of the hypocrisy of liars seared in their own conscience as with a branding iron,** men who forbid marriage and advocate abstaining from foods which God*

---

[143] Jude 4,8-13,16,18-20 NASB

has created to be gratefully shared in by those who believe and know the truth." [144]

The faith community of Jesus must heed these prophetic warnings of these Satanic attacks that will come for one reason only – to deceive the people of God in order to mitigate our effectiveness as God's covenant people, and to, if possible, even deny our faith in Jesus. We must not be ignorant of his schemes because he *"roams about as a roaring lion, seeking whom he may devour."*[145] We must develop an active, vital relationship and communication history with God, as individual followers of Jesus and His faith communities.

Israel Embraces Jesus As Their Messiah

As Jesus neared the time of His crucifixion and resurrection, He taught His disciples what their ministries would be like and the resources that would be made available to them to accomplish these Kingdom activities. Jesus was also confronted, more and more, by the Jewish religious leaders in an effort to trap Him in something He said so they would have grounds to arrest and silence Him.

During one such encounter with these religious leaders, knowing what their aim was and responding to their hypocrisy and efforts to trap Him, Jesus spoke to them and prophesied to the city of Jerusalem, saying:

> *"Jerusalem, Jerusalem, who kills the prophets and stones those who are sent to her! How often I wanted to gather your children together, the way a hen gathers her chicks under her wings, and you were unwilling.* ***Behold, your house is being left to you desolate! For I say to you, from now on you will not see Me until you say,*** *'BLESSED IS HE WHO COMES IN THE NAME OF THE LORD!"* [146]

The religious leaders of the Jewish people, the natural descendants of Abraham and partakers of God's blood covenant with him, had just been rightfully and righteously exposed as being spiritually and

---

144 1Timothy 4:1-3 NASB (emphasis mine)

145 1Peter 5:8-9

146 Matthew 23:37-39 NASB (emphasis mine)

morally bankrupt. They had been rebuked for their spiritual hypocrisy by the very Person who had come to save and restore them to the covenant with God they had broken, time, after time, after time.[147]

Jesus had just pronounced eight "woes" upon these Jewish leaders. A "woe" is, *"a condition of deep suffering from misfortune, affliction, or grief; ruinous trouble."*[148] Jesus told these religious leaders that their outwardly pious appearances and activities are completely superficial and empty because their inward spiritual condition is completely corrupt. It was all an act, to deceive those they led. Punctuating His declaration of woes to these Jewish leaders, Jesus said:

> *"You serpents, you brood of vipers, how will you escape the sentence of hell?"*[149]

Jesus came to speak the words of God and to do the works of God. Yes, Jesus spoke these things to them to condemn their hypocritical words and actions but also to wake them up to where this hypocrisy was leading them. Then, as a final prophetic declaration to the spiritually blind and bankrupt leaders of the Jewish people, Jesus says:

> ***"Behold, your house is being left to you desolate!*** *For I say to you, **from now on you will not see Me until you say, 'BLESSED IS HE WHO COMES IN THE NAME OF THE LORD!'"*** [150]

Jesus, the Messiah, who the Jewish people had been watching and waiting for since He was promised to Abraham by God in His blood covenant with him, is telling the religious leaders that the very temple they revered and cherished would be destroyed and left desolate. Their lack of spiritual honesty and repentance, to acknowledge and embrace Jesus as their promised Messiah, would bring this destruction upon them.[151] This destruction of the Jewish

---

147 Matthew 23:13-33

148 Merriam-Webster Dictionary Online

149 Matthew 23:33 NASB

150 Matthew 23:38-39 NASB (emphasis mine)

151 Luke 19:41-44

temple took place in 70 A.D., by the Romans under the leadership of Titus. No stone of the temple was left standing, one upon another.

Jesus goes on to prophesy that they will not see Him again until they recognize and embrace Him as their Messiah and call out to Him to come to them. This is a critical prophetic event that will occur at *the time of the end*, before Jesus will return to the earth. In that day, the Jewish people and religious leaders in Jerusalem will be persecuted by the Antichrist and False Prophet, and surrounded by their enemies with no allied nations and forces to stand with them against their certain destruction.[152] When they call out to Jesus, recognizing and embracing Him as their Messiah, and ask Him to come and deliver them from their enemies, Jesus will return.

But The People Who Know Their God

The vision and prophecy of Daniel, in chapter 11, gives us wonderful insights into events and activities near *the time of the end.* I mentioned several of them, earlier, but there are a few more that I want to mention here. The angel continues to speak to Daniel, saying:

> *"And such as violate the covenant he shall pervert and seduce with flatteries,* **but the people who know their God shall prove themselves strong and shall stand firm and do exploits [for God].**" *And they who are wise and understanding among the people shall instruct many and make them understand,"* [153]

In the period leading up to *the time of the end,* the followers of Jesus will attain to a proportion of faith and prophetic experience that will enable them to accomplish what Jesus said they would, in His declaration to Peter and the other disciples.[154] Jesus told us that He is restoring humanity to their created place and function as God's representatives and regents on the earth. They will possess the Kingdom authority, ability and tools to successfully accomplish the prophetic activities, on earth, that the Father and Jesus are

---

[152] Luke 21:20; Zechariah 12; Zechariah 14; Joel 3:1-2
[153] Daniel 11:33-35 NASB (emphasis mine)
[154] Matthew 16:17-19

instructing them to do, from heaven. Satan and the domain of darkness will be defeated and will not be able to ultimately overpower or stand against the authority and ability Jesus' followers will possess and exercise, to accomplish these divinely authorized activities.

The second, greater fulfillment of Joel's prophecy will take place at this time, as declared by Peter in Acts 2:

> "*AND IT SHALL BE IN THE LAST DAYS,' God says, 'THAT I WILL POUR FORTH OF MY SPIRIT ON ALL MANKIND; AND YOUR SONS AND YOUR DAUGHTERS SHALL PROPHESY, AND YOUR YOUNG MEN SHALL SEE VISIONS, AND YOUR OLD MEN SHALL DREAM DREAMS; EVEN ON MY BONDSLAVES, BOTH MEN AND WOMEN, I WILL IN THOSE DAYS POUR FORTH OF MY SPIRIT And they shall prophesy. 'AND I WILL GRANT WONDERS IN THE SKY ABOVE AND SIGNS ON THE EARTH BELOW, BLOOD, AND FIRE, AND VAPOR OF SMOKE. 'THE SUN WILL BE TURNED INTO DARKNESS AND THE MOON INTO BLOOD, BEFORE THE GREAT AND GLORIOUS DAY OF THE LORD SHALL COME. 'AND IT SHALL BE THAT EVERYONE WHO CALLS ON THE NAME OF THE LORD WILL BE SAVED.'"* [155]

Even though there was an initial fulfillment of this prophecy; the *early rain*, on the day of Pentecost, the second fulfillment, the *latter rain*, will be fulfilled at the time leading up to the return of Jesus. The followers of Jesus at that time will have gone through God's restoration process and prophetic training. They will be prophetically cooperating with God in order to proclaim and demonstrate the reality of the presence of the Kingdom of God, throughout the earth. God will bear witness with their testimony and this reality with signs and wonders. The followers of Jesus will "*prove themselves strong and shall stand firm and do exploits for God...they who are wise and understanding among the people shall instruct many and make them understand.*" They will grow in their knowledge and understanding of God, the Kingdom of God, and their place in His end time prophetic activities, in the time leading up to *the time of the end.*

---

[155] Acts 2:17-21 NASB (emphasis mine)

An Unprecedented Increase In Travel & Knowledge

Yet, there is more, concerning these end time events and activities, that the angel tells Daniel, and we can find it in Daniel, chapter 12:

> *"Now **at that time** Michael, the great prince who stands guard over the sons of your people, will arise. And **there will be a time of distress such as never occurred since there was a nation until that time;** and at that time your people, **everyone who is found written in the book, will be rescued. Many of those who sleep in the dust of the ground will awake, these to everlasting life**, but the others to disgrace and everlasting contempt. **Those who have insight will shine brightly like the brightness of the expanse of heaven, and those who lead the many to righteousness, like the stars forever and ever**. But as for you, Daniel, conceal these words and seal up the book **until the end of time; many will go back and forth, and knowledge will increase.**"* [156]

In Chapter 12, the angel gives Daniel some of the *"signs of the times"* that give us an indication that we are nearing *the time of the end* and the return of Jesus. The people of God *"who have made themselves ready"* [157] will experience an unprecedented period of prophetic engagement, cooperation and interaction with God as He demonstrates, through them, the presence and reality of His Kingdom on the earth, to the nations of the world. This will occur up to and during a time of distress that humanity has not experienced before. At this time in human history, people will be traveling, extensively, throughout the earth and knowledge will be greatly increasing. At the same time, those who have been given insight into the plans and activities of God will make these insights known to people throughout the earth, and those who lead others to the Kingdom of God will be as numerous *as the stars in the night sky.*

---

[156] Daniel 12:1-4 NASB (emphasis mime)

[157] Luke 12:35-38

Yet, there is another sign of *the time of the end,* which the angel reveals to Daniel, that we will discuss in greater detail in the next chapter. This sign is, *"at that time your people, everyone who is found written in the book, will be rescued. Many of those who sleep in the dust of the ground will awake, these to everlasting life."* Let's take a look at this "harvest" and other Kingdom events that will occur when Jesus returns to establish the complete, visible Kingdom of God on the earth.

- *Takeaways for the reader:*

    o God knows what will take place at the end of the age, and He has given us tremendous insight into these activities and events so we aren't caught unaware when they occur

    o Satan's activities will increase as we draw closer to *the time of the end* but so will God's, and He will demonstrate these prophetic activities through His Kingdom people – His faith community, the Church

    o Satan and the domain of darkness will not be able to defeat God's prophetic faith community, and his "gates" will not be able to withstand the faith-filled, prophetic offensive that the Church engages in against him, as they declare and demonstrate the reality and presence of the Kingdom of God to the people and nations of the earth

    o The Antichrist and the False Prophet will appear in order to deceive the people and nations of the earth. God will allow them to temporarily overcome the followers of Jesus so that the evil, sinful rebellion of humanity against God, which has been increasing throughout human history, can come to its full maturity and measure.

    o There will be a great apostasy or falling away from the faith, by followers of Jesus, as a result of their inability to recognize and resist the deceptive lies of Satan, as they are promoted by those who are devoid of the truth and the Holy Spirit.

- The followers of Jesus will engage in unprecedented prophetic Kingdom activities, supported by the Holy Spirit and signs and wonders by God's hand, in order to demonstrate to the world that the Kingdom of God is present and that they can escape the wrath of God to come, through faith in Jesus

- *Small group questions*:

  - How will God's prophetic training prepare us to recognize the signs of the times, resist the lies and deceptions of Satan, and engage with God in His prophetic Kingdom activities as we draw closer to *the time of the end* and the return of Jesus?

  - How does knowing *the signs of the times* and the events that will happen at *the time of the end* help us in our daily faith experience with God and the events and activities we encounter in our lives? How will it affect our lives if we do not know and understand them, as the Bible explains them?

  - How important is the Holy Spirit to our ability to discern and understand what is going on around us, and how we should respond to events and activities that confront and engage us, every day? How does the Holy Spirit help us to know the will of God, stay "tuned in" to Him, and respond effectively to Him in these situations?

  - Based on what the scriptures tell us, what will the great *falling away from the faith* look like? What will be the major reasons for it? What can we do to protect ourselves and others from these deceptions?

Chapter 8

REGENTS RESURRECTED, RULING & SUBDUING THE EARTH

"Therefore we have been buried with Him through baptism into death, so that as Christ was raised from the dead through the glory of the Father, so we too might walk in newness of life. For if we **have become united with Him in the likeness of His death, certainly we shall also be in the likeness of His resurrection."** Romans 6:4-5 NASB (emphasis mine)

"For this we say to you by the word of the Lord, that we who are alive and remain until the coming of the Lord, will not precede those who have fallen asleep. For the Lord Himself will descend from heaven with a shout, with the voice of the archangel and with the trumpet of God, and **the dead in Christ will rise first. Then we who are alive and remain will be caught up together with them in the clouds to meet the Lord in the air,** *and so we shall always be with the Lord."* 1Thessalonians 4:15-17 NASB (emphasis mine)

"For the anxious longing of the creation waits eagerly for the revealing of the sons of God. *For the creation was subjected to futility, not willingly, but because of Him who subjected it, in hope that* **the creation itself also will be set free from its slavery to corruption into the freedom of the glory of the children of God. For we know that the whole creation groans and suffers the pains of childbirth together until now."** Romans 8:19-22 NASB (emphasis mine)

Jesus is returning to rule the earth as the King of kings and Lord of lords. It's not a matter of *if,* but *when.*

We've identified several of the key events and activities that will occur on the earth in the time leading up to the return of Jesus. In this chapter we are going to look at some of the events and activities that occur when Jesus returns. Before we do, I want to briefly lay a foundation for why these unprecedented events *must* occur. They represent a giant leap forward for humanity in regard to our restoration and the completion of our divine mandate.

We know that humanity rebelled against God and needed restoration to our original condition, position, and mandate with God. We needed a legal substitute to willingly take our divine judgment upon himself, if we are to ever experience what God originally created us to be and do. Jesus willingly became our legal substitute, suffering God's divine judgment for our rebellion, so we can be restored to relationship with God. Jesus, having died, was then resurrected - raised from the dead to newness of life; He will never suffer physical death again. As a result of our identification with and faith in Jesus' substitutionary death, we too, are raised with Him to newness of life.[158] This is what water baptism reminds us of and declares to the world.[159]

Our identification with and faith in the physical resurrection of Jesus from the dead gives us the divine promise that we, too, will experience this same physical resurrection, never to die again. To seal this divine promise, God has given us His Holy Spirit as a down payment – a guarantee that He will physically raise us from the dead at some point in the future.[160] We were spiritually resurrected when we were born again. Yet, until this physical resurrection takes place, we are still subject to weakness and imperfection as a result of the effects of sin upon our physical bodies. For those followers of Jesus who have physically died, they are spiritually present with God in heaven but are without their physical body; it is not yet resurrected. Jesus, as a result of His physical resurrection from the dead, is "the first-born from the dead",[161] "the first-born among of many brethren".[162]

Being *spiritually* resurrected is wonderful but it is incomplete. *We cannot complete our divine mandate, on this physical earth, as spirits without physical bodies that are holy, righteous, immortal and free from the effects of sin.* We must be physically resurrected

---

[158] Romans 6:1-11

[159] Colossians 2:12-14

[160] Ephesians 1:13-14; 2Corinthians 1:22; 2Corinthians 5:5

[161] Revelation 1:4

[162] Romans 8:29

and given an immortal, eternal body that will fully function upon the earth, forever, as God initially created it. This is why God promised to physically resurrect us, giving us the Holy Spirit as His guarantee that it will happen.

This is the backdrop for the events and activities that are going to occur when Jesus returns to the earth. Humanity is going to take a giant leap forward in our restoration process when Jesus returns. Mortality will put on immortality, and we will be changed. [163]

Creation Will Be Released From Its Bondage

Creation, itself, is groaning under the weight and pressure of sin and evil that has increased upon the earth. Scientists, environmentalists and others within the human community have recognized that an upheaval is taking place within the natural, physical environment of the earth but have misdiagnosed the cause. Yes, humanity is at the center of this environmental upheaval, but it is not in the way they suppose. It is sin and its effects upon the earth's functional systems that has steadily produced this environmental *groaning*. I use the word *groaning* to describe this effect because that is what Paul calls it, in Romans 8:

> **"For the anxious longing of the creation waits eagerly for the revealing of the sons of God.** For the creation was subjected to futility, not willingly, but because of Him who subjected it, in hope that **the creation itself also will be set free from its slavery to corruption into the freedom of the glory of the children of God. For we know that the whole creation groans and suffers the pains of childbirth together until now."** [164]

Even in the 1st century A.D., Paul recognized and called out the suffering and groaning that creation was experiencing as a result of sin, and it has been steadily increasing ever since. In the last 100 years, this environmental groaning has increased exponentially, and most people recognize it. The "experts" keep circling the target but refuse to identify and acknowledge the real reason for it. They

---

[163] 1Corinthians 15:53-54

[164] Romans 8:19-22 NASB (emphasis mine)

promote *natural* "band-aid" solutions for the symptoms but there is only one real solution.

Creation is in turmoil and it is, ultimately, a spiritual turmoil. The Biblical remedy is what Paul calls the *"revealing of the sons of God"*. Creation will finally be released from its spiritual bondage and experience its freedom from the effects of sin, when God brings forth *"the glory of the children of God."* Just as God is restoring humanity to our rightful position and function within His Kingdom and creation, this "revelation" and "glorification" of the people of God will bring about the restoration and freedom of creation, itself.

The Return of the King

Jesus and many of the Biblical writers have informed and warned us of the increasing corruption that will take place on the earth, as we draw closer to His return. Satan increases his evil activity in an effort to halt the expansion and activities of the Kingdom of God. He will even use *impostors* to infiltrate the faith community of Jesus in an effort to deceive and corrupt the people of God.[165] Satan wants to deceive and hinder redeemed humanity so we are unable to willfully and faithfully engage and cooperate with God in His end-time spiritual activities.

This is what the "full measure" effects of sin will do to someone, angelic or human. They think they can actually defeat God and forever rule themselves. Jesus already won the war but Satan and those who willfully subject themselves to his influence and activities think they can still win; ultimately defeating God. This "full measure" reprobate condition and related activities of sin by sinful humanity have yet to be entered into and conducted upon the earth but, as we will see, it will be, and God must and will bring His judgment upon it.

God warns evil, rebellious humanity of the folly they are engaged in, trying to release themselves from His "constraints" and "intrusions" into their lives. Through the psalmist, God says:

---

[165] Matthew 24:21-24

"Why are the nations in an uproar and the peoples devising a vain thing? **The kings of the earth take their stand and the rulers take counsel together against the LORD and against His Anointed,** *saying, "Let us tear their fetters apart and cast away their cords from us!"* **He who sits in the heavens laughs, the Lord scoffs at them.** *Then He will speak to them in His anger and terrify them in His fury, saying,* **"But as for Me, I have installed My King upon Zion, My holy mountain."** *"I will surely tell of the decree of the LORD: He said to Me, 'You are My Son, today I have begotten You.* **'Ask of Me, and I will surely give the nations as Your inheritance, and the very ends of the earth as Your possession. 'You shall break them with a rod of iron, You shall shatter them like earthenware.'"** [166]

Nearly 1000 years before the birth of Jesus, the psalmist prophesied concerning the relationship between God the Father and the Messiah, the Son of God, and how the Messiah would be installed by the Father as King and Ruler over the entire earth. The prophecy also describes the conversation between the Father and the Messiah at *the time of the end* – when evil, sinful humanity is devising their plans to overthrow God and His Kingdom.

First of all, God laughs at and mocks them in their folly. Then, as the evil kings, rulers and armies gather together against Him, the Father speaks to them. He tells them that He has already determined who is to rule the earth and He will be installing this Person upon the throne in Jerusalem, very shortly. Giving Jesus His instructions for the upcoming battle with evil humanity and for ruling the earth after His victory, the Father tells Jesus to crush this united human rebellion, forever. Then, He is to rule over the earth, subduing it and bringing it into submission and compliance with the Kingdom of God. God the Father is telling Jesus to begin the necessary activities that will ultimately complete the mandate He gave humanity at their creation.

God told humanity, through the psalmist, over 3000 years ago what is going to happen at *the time of the end*, when Jesus returns to establish the visible, complete Kingdom of God upon the earth.

---

[166] Psalm 2:1-9 NASB (emphasis mine)

There are other scriptures, in the Old Testament and the New Testament, that confirm this reality and give us more detailed information concerning when and how this will occur.

The scriptures tell us of the battles that will occur on the earth at the time of Jesus' return. There will be *natural* battles with natural weapons being used but the major battles will be *spiritual*, with spiritual weapons being used, on both sides. God is currently in the process of restoring His spiritual realities and prophetic activities to the Church so the followers of Jesus can effectively engage and cooperate with Him in these end-time battles, as His earthly regents. Righteous humanity must eventually subdue the earth if our divine mandate is to be completed. We must work and cooperate with God, prophetically, if we are to be successful.

Before these spiritual battles, the gospel of the Kingdom of God will have been proclaimed and demonstrated throughout the whole world, as a witness to all of the nations, by the prophetic followers of Jesus. There will also have been a great persecution of the Church and a "great falling away from the faith" of many of them.[167] At a specific point, God will allow the Antichrist to overcome the followers of Jesus so sin and evil can come to its complete maturity – its full measure, and God will bring His judgment upon it:

> "Then *I saw a beast coming up out of the sea,* having ten horns and seven heads, and on his horns were ten diadems, and *on his heads were blasphemous names... And the dragon gave him his power and his throne and great authority... And the whole earth was amazed and followed after the beast; they worshiped the dragon because he gave his authority to the beast;* and they worshiped the beast, saying, "Who is like the beast, and who is able to wage war with him?"... *It was also given to him to make war with the saints and to overcome them,* and authority over every tribe and people and tongue and nation was given to him. All who dwell on the earth will worship him, everyone whose name has not been written from the foundation of the world in the book of life of the Lamb who has been slain."[168]

---

[167] Matthew 24:9-14; 2Thessalonians 2:1-3

"The beast which was and is not, is himself also an eighth and is one of the seven, and he goes to destruction. The ten horns which you saw are ten kings who have not yet received a kingdom, but they receive authority as kings with the beast for one hour. **These have one purpose, and they give their power and authority to the beast. These will wage war against the Lamb, and the Lamb will overcome them, because He is Lord of lords and King of kings, and those who are with Him are the called and chosen and faithful.**" [169]

John saw the Antichrist, the Beast, coming up out of the sea. Many times, when a prophetic scripture refers to a sea or other large body of water without giving it a specific name, the body of water is referring to a sea of people or the human population. The Antichrist rises out of the sea of humanity; he is a human being and a political figure who is actively opposed to God, the Church, and the Jewish people. As a result, Satan (the dragon) delegates his authority and power to the Antichrist. The evil, rebellious people on the earth will worship and follow Satan and the Antichrist. This is when God allows the Antichrist to temporarily overcome the followers of Jesus and to seize control of the nations and armies of the earth.

It is, also, at this time that God removes the restraint of national human governments upon Satan's efforts to unite humanity under one human government against God and the Kingdom of God.[170] God imposed this "dividing" governmental restraint upon humanity in Genesis 11, so a united humanity would not rise up against Him, again, in complete rebellion.[171] Now, evil, wicked humanity and their national governments willingly choose to unite, as one, behind the Antichrist, against God. They are filling up their sin and evil to the full measure before the judgment of God comes upon them.

Followers of Jesus are still on the earth at this time, though many have been martyred for their faith. The Holy Spirit is still working

---

[168] Revelation 13:1-8 NASB (emphasis mine)

[169] Revelation 17:11-14 NASB (emphasis mine)

[170] 2Thessalonians 2:3-7

[171] Genesis 11:1-9

and moving prophetically through them, throughout the earth. We must remember that as a condition for completing our mandate, humanity was commanded by God to, "...*fill the earth and subdue it.*" Again, the Hebrew word for *subdue* is *kabash*. It means to *bring into bondage, make subservient, dominate, tread down.*[172] In order for righteous humanity to complete our mandate, we must be *physically* upon the earth to completely subdue it. This will include subduing Satan, the domain and powers of darkness, as well as evil, defiant and rebellious humanity.

The Resurrection Of Redeemed Humanity

Subduing the earth and completing their mandate is humanity's responsibility. Jesus, the God-Man, who is fully human and received His eternal, immortal body upon His resurrection from the dead, will lead righteous humanity in this endeavor to secure the earth for the Kingdom of God.

This raises the question, "*If evil, rebellious humanity is physically on the earth and righteous, restored humanity are spirit beings in heaven (with the exception of those still living on the earth), how is this battle for possession of the earth supposed to occur?*" Paul gives us insight into how this earthly battle occurs and how it is fought. In 1Corinthians, Paul tells us:

> "*Behold, I tell you a mystery;* **we will not all sleep**, *but* **we will all be changed**, *in a moment, in the twinkling of an eye, at the last trumpet; for the trumpet will sound, and the dead will be raised imperishable, and we will be changed.* For this perishable **must** put on the imperishable, and this mortal **must** put on immortality." [173]

Likewise, in his first letter to the Thessalonians, Paul tells us:

> "*For this we say to you by the word of the Lord, that* **we who are alive and remain until the coming of the Lord**, *will not precede those who have fallen asleep.*

---

[172] The New American Standard Old Testament Hebrew Lexicon

[173] 1Corinthians 15:51-53 NASB (emphasis mine)

For the Lord Himself will descend from heaven with a shout, with the voice of the archangel and with the trumpet of God, and the dead in Christ will rise first. Then we who are alive and remain will be caught up together with them in the clouds to meet the Lord in the air, and so we shall always be with the Lord." [174]

Paul tells us that before this battle for the earth can be fought, righteous, restored humanity *must* receive their physical, immortal bodies; *they must be physically resurrected.* Even those of His followers who are still on the earth when Jesus returns will be resurrected, receiving their eternal, immortal body in place of their mortal body. Paul even gives us the process, order and timing of how this physical resurrection is to occur:

- When Jesus leaves heaven to return to the earth, His followers who have physically died and are in heaven will leave heaven with Him. As they return to Earth with Jesus, they will receive their resurrected, immortal physical bodies to engage and interact with the earth and the people of the earth.
- Those followers of Jesus who are physically alive on the earth at His return, will be changed, in a moment; their mortal bodies will be changed into eternal, immortal bodies as they are caught up to meet Jesus and His other followers in the air, and will turn around to return to the earth with them

There is some confusion among the followers of Jesus in regard to this event. To understand what Paul is saying here, we must understand the customs and manners of the day, as well as the language in which Paul is writing. According to this scripture in 1Thessalonians, in the statement *"Then we who are alive and remain will be caught up to* **meet** *the Lord in the air"*, the Greek word for "meet" is *apantésis*, which means *"the act of meeting, to meet, (a phrase seemingly almost technical for the reception of a newly arrived official)"*.[175] It refers to a singular event where a person or a group of people go out to meet, celebrate, and welcome a dignitary or high government official, and return with him to where

---

[174] 1Thessalonans 4:15-17 NASB (emphasis mine)
[175] Strong's Concordance - Strong's Greek 529

they came from. It does not mean to go out and meet him and return with him to where he came from.

In this scripture, Paul is telling us that when Jesus returns to the earth, at the end of this present age, His followers (those who are alive on the earth at His coming) will go out to the atmosphere surrounding the earth to receive their resurrected bodies and to meet, celebrate, and welcome Jesus. Then, they will turn around and return with Jesus and those resurrected followers who came with Him from heaven, to the earth where they will always be with Him.

Paul goes on to confirm this singular event in 2Thessalonians 1, where he says:

> *"These will pay the penalty of eternal destruction, away from the presence of the Lord and from the glory of His power, **when He comes to be glorified in His saints on that day, and to be marveled at among all who have believed.**"* [176]

In biblical times, when a king returned to his home country and domain, after being away for an extended period of time, it was customary for the citizens of His domain to go out and meet him, often lining the roads that he would travel, and to join him in his return. This celebrated return would often take place throughout the entire land and over a period of time, so all of the citizens, throughout the country, could participate by going out to meet, celebrate, and welcome the king upon his return.

This event, the return of Jesus to the earth, brings about the physical resurrection of righteous humanity, in heaven and on earth. The battle for the earth between evil, rebellious humanity, and redeemed, immortal humanity will take place at the end of this age, at the end of the Tribulation period. It will be the beginning of the completion of humanity's divine mandate. In the book of Revelation, John tells us:

> *"But **immediately after the tribulation of those days** THE SUN WILL BE DARKENED, AND THE MOON WILL NOT*

---

[176] 2Thessalonians 1:9-10 NASB (emphasis mine)

*GIVE ITS LIGHT, AND THE STARS WILL FALL from the sky, and the powers of the heavens will be shaken. And then the sign of the Son of Man will appear in the sky, and **then all the tribes of the earth will mourn, and they will see the SON OF MAN COMING ON THE CLOUDS OF THE SKY with power and great glory. And He will send forth His angels with A GREAT TRUMPET and THEY WILL GATHER TOGETHER His elect from the four winds, from one end of the sky to the other.***" [177]

*"And I saw heaven opened, and behold, a white horse, and He who sat on it is called Faithful and True, and in righteousness He judges and wages war. His eyes are a flame of fire, and on His head are many diadems; and He has a name written on Him which no one knows except Himself. He is clothed with a robe dipped in blood, and His name is called The Word of God. **And the armies which are in heaven, clothed in fine linen, white and clean, were following Him on white horses. From His mouth comes a sharp sword, so that with it He may strike down the nations, and He will rule them with a rod of iron; and He treads the wine press of the fierce wrath of God, the Almighty.** And on His robe and on His thigh He has a name written, "KING OF KINGS, AND LORD OF LORDS.""* [178]

The return of Jesus to the earth will not be in a moment. The physical resurrection of righteous humanity who are on the earth will be in a moment. The return of Jesus to the earth will take place over a period of time and will encompass the entire earth, as *"all eyes will see Him"* [179]. Jesus and His resurrected followers will circle the earth as they return, where everyone on the earth will see Him as He returns in all of His glory. Even the kings and nations of the earth, who have chosen to follow the Antichrist and Satan, will see Him and they will take action to gather and meet Him in battle when He arrives. [180] John tells us, in the book of Revelation:

---

[177] Matthew 24:29-31 NASB (emphasis mine)

[178] Revelation 19:11-16 NASB (emphasis mine)

[179] Revelation 1:7

[180] Revelation 16:13-16

*"Then I saw an angel standing in the sun, and he cried out with a loud voice, saying to all the birds which fly in midheaven, "Come, assemble for the great supper of God, so that you may eat the flesh of kings and the flesh of commanders and the flesh of mighty men and the flesh of horses and of those who sit on them and the flesh of all men, both free men and slaves, and small and great." **And I saw the beast and the kings of the earth and their armies assembled to make war against Him who sat on the horse and against His army. And the beast was seized, and with him the false prophet who performed the signs in his presence, by which he deceived those who had received the mark of the beast and those who worshiped his image; these two were thrown alive into the lake of fire which burns with brimstone. And the rest were killed with the sword which came from the mouth of Him who sat on the horse, and all the birds were filled with their flesh."** [181]*

The kings and armies of the earth will see Jesus returning with His armies of followers and will gather to meet them in battle when they arrive. This gathering and assembling of armies and war assets is not accomplished in a moment. It doesn't happen instantaneously. It takes a period of time, perhaps two to three weeks, for the kings and armies of the earth to physically assemble in one, specific place to engage Jesus and His followers in battle. These kings and armies are led by Satan and the Antichrist and they are convinced that this battle is for the permanent control of the earth and of all humanity. Every person on the earth sees Jesus and His followers as they are returning. They know, exactly, what is about to happen when He gets here. They aren't caught in a surprise attack by Jesus. Jesus takes His time coming, allowing everyone on the earth to see Him, and the kings and armies of the earth to gather and assemble against Him.

The battle between the kings and armies of the earth, and Jesus, with His immortal, human army, is not a long battle. The Antichrist and the False Prophet are defeated and cast alive into the Lake of Fire. The assembled kings and armies of evil, rebellious humanity

---

[181] Revelation 19:17-21 NASB (emphasis mine)

are destroyed by the word of God coming from Jesus' mouth. This is how nonsensical the plan of Satan is, as well as the efforts of rebellious humanity to achieve permanent, personal rulership of the earth and their lives. God always wins. The plan of God and His plan for humanity will be accomplished. Humanity will complete our divine mandate – our great commission. This victory to establish the visible, complete Kingdom of God on the earth is but Phase 1 in the plan to complete the mandate. The battle of this age, for control of the earth, is over but righteous humanity must still govern the entire earth and ensure that it is completely subdued before the mandate is completed.

- *Takeaways for the reader*:

  o The followers of Jesus will perform tremendous signs and wonders by the Holy Spirit as the proclaim the reality and presence of the Kingdom of God to the people and nations of the world. Many of them will be martyred and the Antichrist will be allowed to temporarily overcome them, so the sin and evil within rebellious humanity can come to maturity – achieve its full measure.

  o Redeemed humanity must possess physical bodies if they are to successfully live on, rule over, and subdue the earth. They can't achieve this while living as spirit beings in heaven. Therefore, they must be physically resurrected and given immortal, physical bodies in which they will live and serve God, on the earth, forever.

  o Creation "groans" as a result of the effects of sin. It waits for the glorification of the sons of God to be set free from its slavery. When redeemed humanity is resurrected and glorified, and they establish the complete, visible Kingdom of God on the earth, creation is set free from its slavery, as well.

  o At the end of the Tribulation Period, Jesus returns to the earth and resurrects righteous humanity: the dead in Christ will physically rise first, to join with their spirits that are returning with Jesus; then those alive on the earth at His coming will be resurrected and will join Jesus and the rest of immortal humanity in the air, as they all return to the earth to establish the Kingdom of God upon it.

o The return of Jesus will take time, so everyone on the earth can see Him as He returns, and so the kings and armies of the earth can assemble in one place to engage Him in battle when He arrives.

o Jesus and resurrected humanity defeat the Antichrist and the armies of the earth. The Antichrist and the False Prophet are thrown into the Lake of Fire, and the armies of the earth are completely destroyed by Jesus and His followers.

- *Small group questions*:

o Before the return of Jesus, God will confront sinful humanity with the reality of His Kingdom and its presence with signs, wonders and miracles through His Kingdom people, as they declare this reality. What can we do, now, to prepare to engage and cooperate with God in these prophetic Kingdom activities, as individuals and as a faith community, when that time comes?

o Knowing that many of the followers of Jesus around the world will lose their lives, as they willingly engage in God's Kingdom activities and proclaim the presence of His Kingdom to those around them, what can we do to prepare ourselves for such an experience, and how will this impact how we engage in our faith experience with God, moving forward?

o Knowing what is coming upon the world in *the time of the end*, what can we do to encourage those around us to consider this reality and respond to Jesus with humility and faith? Sinful humanity gives little attention to and is impacted very little by the message of Jesus Christ, today. Why do you think that is, and what can we do about it?

CHAPTER 9

OUR MANDATE COMPLETED

"And **the wolf will dwell with the lamb,** and **the leopard will lie down with the young goat,** and **the calf and the young lion and the fatling together;** and **a little boy will lead them.** Also, **the cow and the bear will graze, their young will lie down together,** and **the lion will eat straw like the ox. The nursing child will play by the hole of the cobra,** and **the weaned child will put his hand on the viper's den. They will not hurt or destroy in all My holy mountain,** for **the earth will be full of the knowledge of the LORD as the waters cover the sea.**" Isaiah 11:6-9 – NASB (emphasis mine)

"**When the thousand years are completed, Satan will be released from his prison, and will come out to deceive the nations which are in the four corners of the earth,** Gog and Magog, **to gather them together for the war; the number of them is like the sand of the seashore.** And they came up on the broad plain of the earth and surrounded the camp of the saints and the beloved city, and **fire came down from heaven and devoured them. And the devil who deceived them was thrown into the lake of fire and brimstone, where the beast and the false prophet are also; and <u>they will be tormented day and night forever and ever.</u>**" Revelation 20:7-10 – NASB (emphasis mine)

Righteous humanity's physical resurrection to eternal, immortal bodies will be a giant leap forward in regard to completing our divine mandate. Jesus, accompanied by His righteous, resurrected followers returns to the earth to "*slay the wicked with the breath of His mouth*" and to "*rule with a rod of iron*". This event is the first major activity by immortal humanity to establish the physical reign of God upon the earth and actually subdue it. *Ruling over* and *subduing the entire earth* are two necessary conditions of the original mandate humanity must complete. Jesus, the God-Man, who is fully human, leads resurrected humanity to complete these two very important conditions. Yet, neither of them is entirely completed at Jesus' return. There is still much work to accomplish.

Jesus and His followers return to fight the battle for dominion over the earth. The Antichrist and the False Prophet are defeated. This is where we see the scriptures starting to be fulfilled that speak of Jesus and righteous humanity *"ruling with a rod of iron"*.

It is important to understand what this means if we are to understand our mission upon the earth, when we "reclaim" it for the Kingdom of God. This *ruling with a rod of iron* actually takes place in two phases: 1) when Jesus and His followers return to the earth to defeat the Antichrist, the False Prophet, and the evil, rebellious kings and armies gathered against them; and 2) when Jesus and His followers establish their regency rule upon the earth over the members of rebellious humanity who survive the tribulation period and the battle for dominion over the earth.

Throughout the scriptures, God has established this truth and it is now coming to pass; it is being restored:

> *"Then a shoot will spring from the stem of Jesse, and a branch from his roots will bear fruit. The Spirit of the LORD will rest on Him, the spirit of wisdom and understanding, the spirit of counsel and strength, the spirit of knowledge and the fear of the LORD.* **And He will delight in the fear of the LORD, and He will not judge by what His eyes see, nor make a decision by what His ears hear; but with righteousness He will judge the poor, and decide with fairness for the afflicted of the earth; and He will strike the earth with the rod of His mouth, and with the breath of His lips He will slay the wicked.** *Also, righteousness will be the belt about His loins, and faithfulness the belt about His waist."* [182]

---

[182] Isaiah 11:1-5 NASB (emphasis mine)

"Nevertheless, what you have, hold fast until I come. **He who overcomes, and he who keeps My deeds until the end, TO HIM I WILL GIVE AUTHORITY OVER THE NATIONS; AND HE SHALL RULE THEM WITH A ROD OF IRON, AS THE VESSELS OF THE POTTER ARE BROKEN TO PIECES,** *as I also have received authority from My Father."* [183]

God has decreed that Jesus and righteous, resurrected humanity will be given authority over the evil, rebellious nations of humanity upon the earth, and we shall *"rule them with a rod of iron"*. Jesus will slay the wicked *"with the breath of His lips"*. To confirm this, there is a scripture in Luke 19, where Jesus is using a parable to teach His disciples to be faithful and trustworthy with the Kingdom realities and resources they are entrusted with during their faith experience with Him. In this parable, Jesus explains what the Kingdom of God is like and how it functions, especially as it relates to His return to heaven for a period of time, and His eventual return to the earth to rule over and subdue it. In this scripture, Jesus tells us:

"While they were listening to these things, Jesus went on to tell a parable, because He was near Jerusalem, and they supposed that the kingdom of God was going to appear immediately. So, He said, "A nobleman went to a distant country **to receive a kingdom for himself,** *and then return."...* **"But his citizens hated him and sent a delegation after him, saying, 'We do not want this man to reign over us.' When he returned, after receiving the kingdom,** *he ordered that these slaves, to whom he had given the money, be called to him so that he might know what business they had done."..."I tell you that to everyone who has, more shall be given, but from the one who does not have, even what he does have shall be taken away.* **"But these enemies of mine, who did not want me to reign over them, bring them here and slay them in my presence."** [184]

This scripture, and others, describe what Jesus will do when He reigns upon the earth. Revelation 19 tells us:

---

[183] Revelation 2:25-27 NASB (emphasis mine)
[184] Luke 19:11-12,14-15,26-27 NASB (emphasis mine)

*"From His mouth comes a sharp sword, so **that with it He may strike down the nations,** and **He will rule them with a rod of iron; and He treads the wine press of the fierce wrath of God, the Almighty.**"* [185]

Jesus, when He returns to the earth, must do battle with those who have threatened to deny or usurp His governing authority. The rod of iron is the rule of justice and judgment, and Jesus will return to the earth to bring the justice and judgment of God upon those on the earth who resist and deny His rule. Immortal humanity returns with Jesus to crush the rebellion of sinful humanity and to bring the righteous reign of God to bear upon the earth. This is a vital part of governing and this is the first act of governance that Jesus and His followers enact, upon their return.

The Antichrist and the False Prophet are defeated and thrown, physically, into the *Lake of Fire* where they will remain forever and ever. The Antichrist is the human leader of the Satanic, corrupt *political* system that is overthrown by Jesus, and the False Prophet is the human leader of the Satanic, corrupt *religious* system that is overthrown, at that same time:

> *"**And the beast was seized, and with him the false prophet** who performed the signs in his presence, by which he deceived those who had received the mark of the beast and those who worshiped his image; **these two were thrown alive into the lake of fire** which burns with brimstone."* [186]

Even though the Antichrist and the False Prophet are taken and thrown, physically, into the Lake of Fire, forever, the job of subduing the entire earth is not complete. We know that upon the arrival of Jesus and His followers to the earth, the kings and armies of the earth who were gathered against them to wage war are completely destroyed by the word of God proceeding from Jesus' mouth:

> *"And **the rest were killed with the sword which came from the mouth of Him who sat on the horse,***

---

[185] Revelation 19:15 NASB (emphasis mine)

[186] Revelation 19:20 NASB (emphasis mine)

*and **all the birds were filled with their flesh.***" [187]

These national rulers and governments give their authority to the Antichrist to lead evil, rebellious humanity to wage war with Jesus for dominion of the earth. Yet, what about the people who remain after the battle? Most of the remaining people will have received the mark of the beast and must be immediately judged and executed, as Jesus described in His parable. John describes it this way:

> *"Then another angel, a third one, followed them, saying with a loud voice, **"If anyone worships the beast and his image, and receives a mark on his forehead or on his hand, he also will drink of the wine of the wrath of God, which is mixed in full strength in the cup of His anger; and he will be tormented with fire and brimstone in the presence of the holy angels and in the presence of the Lamb.** "And the smoke of their torment goes up forever and ever; they have no rest day and night,* those who worship the beast and his image, and whoever receives the mark of his name."""* [188]

Yet, all of unredeemed humanity is not destroyed upon Jesus' return. Many people do not receive the mark of the Antichrist and will survive the various plagues and bowls containing God's wrath. Jesus and His followers will rule and govern these remaining people with a rod of iron. They will live into the 1,000-year period of Jesus' reign if they willingly subject themselves to the rule of the Kingdom of God.

In addition to these ruling and governing activities, what happens to Satan when Jesus returns? We are told that he is not immediately imprisoned forever but will be unable to influence sinful humanity and the affairs of earth, for a time:

> *"Then I saw an angel coming down from heaven, holding the key of the abyss and a great chain in his hand. And **he laid hold of the dragon, the serpent of old, who is the devil and Satan, and bound him for a thousand years; and he threw him into the abyss, and***

---

[187] Revelation 19:21 NASB (emphasis mine)
[188] Revelation 14:9-11 NASB (emphasis mine)

shut it and sealed it over him, so that he would not deceive the nations any longer, until the thousand years were completed; after these things he must be released for a short time." [189]

Jesus and righteous humanity vanquish the human perpetrators of the recent rebellion, and Satan is held in the abyss for the 1000 years of Jesus reign, until he is temporarily released. Yet, there still remains the need to subdue those of rebellious humanity who carry over from their corrupt governments and cultures. Even though the remaining people weren't destroyed, they still possess the sin nature and accompanying attitudes and actions that can and will corrupt a people and culture unless they are subdued.

These unredeemed people will experience the government of God as it is established upon the earth. What begins, now, is the active rule of God's regents over the entire earth, under the leadership of Jesus, the son of God and the son of David:

> *"Then I saw thrones, and they sat on them, and judgment was given to them. And I saw the souls of those who had been beheaded because of their testimony of Jesus and because of the word of God, and those who had not worshiped the beast or his image, and had not received the mark on their forehead and on their hand; and they came to life and reigned with Christ for a thousand years."* [190]

And, as Jesus had promised those who willingly choose to follow Him during their faith experience with Him upon the earth:

> *"He who overcomes, I will grant to him to sit down with Me on My throne, as I also overcame and sat down with My Father on His throne. He who has an ear, let him hear what the Spirit says to the churches."'* [191]

The New Jerusalem

---

[189] Revelation 20:1-3 NASB (emphasis mine)
[190] Revelation 20:4 NASB (emphasis mine)
[191] Revelation 3:21-22 NASB (emphasis mine)

The earth and the mortal people who inhabit it will be subject to the reign of God through Jesus and righteous, immortal humanity for 1,000 years. God tells us what it will be like as the government of Jesus rebuilds the cities of the earth after their destruction during the Tribulation period. The lives of the people who remain are transitioned from the domain of darkness and sin to the righteous culture of the Kingdom of God:

> *"Great is the LORD, and greatly to be praised, in* **the city of our God, His holy mountain. <u>Beautiful in elevation, the joy of the whole earth</u>,** *is Mount Zion in the far north,* **the city of the great King**... <u>*As we have heard, so have we seen*</u> *in the city of the LORD of hosts, in the city of our God;* **<u>God will establish her forever</u>**.*"* [192]

> *"Now it will come about that in the last days* **<u>the mountain of the house of the LORD</u> will be established as the chief of the mountains,** *and* <u>**will be raised above the hills**</u>; **and all the nations will stream to it.** *And* **many peoples will come and say, "Come, <u>let us go up to the mountain of the LORD, to the house of the God of Jacob</u>**; *that He may teach us concerning His ways and that we may walk in His paths."* **For the law will go forth from Zion and the word of the LORD from Jerusalem.** *And He will judge between the nations, and will render decisions for many peoples;* and **they will hammer their swords into plowshares and their spears into pruning hooks. Nation will not lift up sword against nation, and <u>never again will they learn war</u>**.*"* [193]

These scriptures, and many more, describe the reign of Jesus and His followers during these 1000 years. What is *"the mountain of the house of the Lord, the house of the God of Jacob"* this scripture is talking about? What is it about Jerusalem, at this time, that the people of the earth will say to one another, *"As we have heard so have we seen"*? How will it be *"beautiful in elevation"*, *"the joy of the whole earth"*, *"raised above the hills"*? We are told that *"the*

---

[192] Psalm 42:1,2,8 NASB (emphasis mine)
[193] Isaiah 2:2-4 NASB (emphasis mine)

nations will stream to it", and the people will say to one another, *"let us go...that He may teach us concerning His ways and that we may walk in His paths."*

It is clear from these scriptures that something unique takes place in Jerusalem when Jesus begins to rule the earth; that sets the location of His rule and reign apart from what already exists, there. It is elevated. It is raised above the hills that currently surround Jerusalem. The people from around the world will have heard of it but when they travel there, they will see it. The nations will stream to it so that Jesus will teach them His ways; so they may walk in His paths. What is it about Jerusalem that will be changed from what it is now, and will be the talk of all of the nations?

Jesus, during His earthly ministry, gave us a hint. Shortly before Jesus is to go to the cross, He meets with His disciples and tells them many things concerning the Kingdom of God, the Holy Spirit, the nature and results of their ministries, and about what awaits them in the future. It is at this time that Jesus encourages them, and us, by saying:

> *"Do not let your heart be troubled; believe in God, believe also in Me. **In My Father's house are many dwelling places**; if it were not so, I would have told you; **for I go to prepare a place for you**. If I go and prepare a place for you, **I will come again and receive you to Myself, that where I am, there you may be also**."* [194]

Jesus tells His disciples that where God is, in heaven, there are many dwelling places or places of residence. Jesus says that He is going to heaven to prepare places of residence for them, and for us, as His Kingdom people. When He returns to the earth, He will receive us to Himself, where we will remain with Him, forever. We tend to read this scripture and imagine what it will be like to live with Jesus in heaven, in our own place of residence that He is preparing for each of us, there.

Yet, when Jesus comes to receive us to Himself, He and we are not in heaven. We are in the atmosphere surrounding the earth, and we are being joined with our resurrected, immortal bodies to return to

---

[194] John 14:1-3 NASB (emphasis mine)

the earth to rule it for 1000 years. We aren't in heaven and will never reside in heaven, again. In fact, those followers of Jesus who are on the earth at His return, will never reside in heaven. They will be caught up to meet Him in the air and then return with Him to the earth. So, *"where He is"* and *"where we will also be"* is not in heaven. We will always be with Him upon the earth, at His return.

Jesus was going to heaven to prepare a place for us to dwell with Him *on the earth.* This "place" where we will dwell with Jesus on the earth must be in Jerusalem because that is the location of His throne and where He will be. What kind of place will this be? It must be able to accommodate billions of His followers, who will have their own, individual dwelling place or place of residence. Where will we find such a place in the city of Jerusalem that will accommodate billions of resurrected human beings, forever?

It is called the *New Jerusalem.* We will live within it during the 1000-year reign of Jesus, on this present earth, as well as upon the new earth after this present earth is destroyed and replaced. Here is John's description of it:

> *"I saw the holy city,* **new Jerusalem,** *coming down out of heaven from God, made ready as a bride adorned for her husband." "Then one of the seven angels who had the seven bowls full of the seven last plagues came and spoke with me, saying, "Come here, I will show you the bride, the wife of the Lamb.* **And he carried me away in the Spirit to a great and high mountain, and showed me the holy city, Jerusalem, coming down out of heaven from God, having the glory of God.** *Her brilliance was like a very costly stone, as a stone of crystal-clear jasper.* **It had a great and high wall, with twelve gates, and at the gates twelve angels; and names were written on them, which are the names of the twelve tribes of the sons of Israel.** *There were three gates on the east and three gates on the north and three gates on the south and three gates on the west.* **And the wall of the city had twelve foundation stones, and on them were the twelve names of the twelve apostles of the Lamb.** *The one who spoke with me had a gold measuring rod to measure the city, and its gates and its wall.* **The city is laid out as a square, and its length is as great as the**

width; and he measured the city with the rod,
fifteen hundred miles; its length and width and
height are equal." [195]

This is the "dwelling place" that Jesus returned to heaven to prepare for us, that *"where He is, we may be, also"*. The new Jerusalem is where glorified humanity will live, forever. This will be our place of residence upon the earth during the 1000-year reign, and beyond. The city is built as a residence that will house billions of people who will rule the earth at Jesus' side during the 1,000-year reign. The rebellious people who survive the Tribulation period will not live here but will live throughout the earth, as humanity always has. They will be responsible for restoring and rebuilding the earth's cities, resources, and infrastructure, within the culture of the Kingdom of God and under the rule of Jesus.

There are many characteristics about the new Jerusalem that are unfathomable. Yet, there is one characteristic that I want to focus on, right now, and that is the size of the city. In Revelation 21 we are told that the city is 1,500 miles long, 1,500 miles wide, and 1,500 miles high – it is a 1,500-mile cube. Think about that. Jesus and immortal humanity will rule the earth from what is present-day Jerusalem. This new Jerusalem will come down to the earth from heaven and will remain where present-day Jerusalem is located. If we look at a map of the Middle East, specifically in the area where the current city of Jerusalem and the nation of Israel are located, we will see a troubling fact.

The nation of Israel, today, is only 263 miles long and 71 miles wide at their longest and widest points, with the metropolitan area of Jerusalem occupying only 48 square miles within Israel. The 1,500-mile cube of new Jerusalem will obviously not fit within the boundaries of Jerusalem or of Israel. The entire Middle East region measures approximately 1,800 miles long and 1,900 miles wide. The new Jerusalem would fill almost the entire area of the Middle East. The earth's atmosphere is approximately 300 miles thick. Therefore, the new Jerusalem will extend 1,200 miles into what we know as "outer space".

The new Jerusalem, when it comes down from God out of heaven,

---

[195] Revelation 21:2,9-16 NASB (emphasis mine)

will be nearly as large as the entire Middle East and will extend far into outer space. The weight of it, especially when it is occupied by billions of people, would crush everything that occupies the Middle East area. How can we rule the earth from Jerusalem when Jerusalem, Israel, and everything within 1,500 miles is covered and crushed by it? Also, can you imagine how long it would take the residents of the new Jerusalem to ascend and descend the 1,500 miles within the city, to go to and from the earth, even if we were to use the most modern elevator technology to do so?

I highlight these astounding facts as a way of emphasizing the sheer enormity of the new Jerusalem and that it must be in close proximity to the current city of Jerusalem. Yet, God is very aware of these potential challenges and has already taken them, and many others, into account when He designed and prepared the city for its eternal purpose and placement.

The scripture in Revelation 21 describes the new Jerusalem descending to the earth but says nothing about it resting upon the earth. It also tells us that it already possesses its foundation when it descends; it does not need a foundation prepared for it upon the earth. The stones of the foundation bear the names of the twelve apostles of Jesus. I don't believe there is a rock formation or any other sort of "natural" foundation that can adequately support the weight and dimensions of a city that is a 1,500-mile cube.

This city will not rest upon the earth but will be suspended above the earth. God will, by His great power, cause the new Jerusalem to hover above the earth, and there will be an effective means for its residents to go back and forth within the city, as well as to and from the earth. We will have our immortal, glorified bodies at that time and if they are anything like Jesus' glorified body after His physical resurrection, moving around in a timely and efficient manner will not be a problem. [196]

The Marriage Supper of the Lamb & The Judgment Seat of Christ

Later in this chapter we will discuss what is known as the judgment of unrighteous, rebellious humanity before the throne of God, when

---

[196] Luke 24:13-31; John 20:19-29

the books are open and they are judged according to their deeds. What I want to briefly cover here is another judgment that will occur within the human family; what the Bible refers to as the *judgment seat of Christ*.[197] This is the judgment or evaluation, by Jesus, of righteous, redeemed humanity and our activities of faith that took place during our lives upon the earth.

The Bible doesn't give us a firm time for when this *Judgment Seat* evaluation by Jesus occurs. Yet, if we look at the scriptural events that take place at *the time of the end* and into the millennial reign of Jesus, I believe we can estimate as to when this event occurs. There are some within the Church who believe that the judgment seat of Christ occurs, individually, upon the physical death of each believer when they get to heaven. I disagree with this position because not all believers will go to heaven when they die, namely, those who are alive on the earth and "caught up" to meet Jesus in the air, when He returns.

I believe the Judgment Seat evaluation is *an event* that begins at a specific time and occurs over a period of time, considering there will be billions of His followers who will be individually evaluated. These evaluations will begin and occur after all righteous, redeemed people have completed their earthly, mortal lives.

Jesus' parable supports this time frame for the Judgment Seat of Christ event taking place upon the earth, after His return:

> *"**A nobleman went to a distant country to receive a kingdom for himself, and then return.** And he called ten of his slaves, and gave them ten minas and said to them, 'Do business with this **until I come back**.' But his citizens hated him and sent a delegation after him, saying, 'We do not want this man to reign over us.' **When he returned, after receiving the kingdom**, he ordered that these slaves, to whom he had given the money, be called to him so that he might know what business they had done."*[198]

A Bride Adorned For Her Husband

---

[197] 2Corinthians 5:9-11
[198] Luke 19:12-15 NASB (emphasis mine)

Subsequent to this event, there is another event involving Jesus and the entire redeemed community that will occur after they have all completed their earthly, mortal lives. This event is the *Marriage Supper of the Lamb.* The Bible doesn't precisely tell us when this event will take place, either, other than there is a declaration made concerning those who receive an invitation to attend it, shortly before Jesus returns to the earth:

> *"Let us rejoice and be glad and give the glory to Him, for* **the marriage of the Lamb has come and His bride has made herself ready.** *" It was given to her to clothe herself in fine linen, bright and clean; for the fine linen is the righteous acts of the saints. Then he said to me, "Write,* **'Blessed are those who are invited to the marriage supper of the Lamb.** '" *And he said to me, "These are true words of God."... And* **I saw heaven opened, and behold, a white horse, and He who sat on it is called Faithful and True, and in righteousness He judges and wages war.** *His eyes are a flame of fire, and on His head are many diadems; and He has a name written on Him which no one knows except Himself. He is clothed with a robe dipped in blood, and His name is called The Word of God.* **And the armies which are in heaven, clothed in fine linen, white and clean, were following Him on white horses.** *"* [199]

The *Marriage Supper of the Lamb* will not occur in heaven, before Jesus returns to the earth, because there are still members of the redeemed community living on the earth at His coming. All of God's people must be present for the *Marriage Supper* to occur and this is not possible until after Jesus returns to the earth to establish His reign. Those on the earth will be caught up to meet Him in the air and will return with Jesus, along with the rest of immortal humanity who came from heaven with Him.

Based on the necessary events that must occur, and the order and timing of those events, it is my conviction that the *Judgment Seat* (evaluation) *of Christ* and the *Marriage Supper of the Lamb* will both occur on the earth, shortly after Jesus has defeated the armies

---

[199] Revelation 19:7-14 NASB (emphasis mine)

of unrighteous humanity and has begun to reign as King. All of righteous humanity will possess their immortal, glorified bodies and they will all live together with Jesus in the new Jerusalem. Jesus will, then, conduct His evaluation of each follower's life of faith, while living in their mortal body, and will present them with their rewards upon its completion. Once Jesus completes these evaluations and they receive their rewards, the *Marriage Supper of the Lamb*, with His Bride in attendance, will occur.

Our Faith & Expectations Are Rewarded

Concerning the *Judgment Seat of Christ*, Paul tells us:

> *"Therefore we also have as our ambition, whether at home or absent, to be pleasing to Him.* ***For we must all appear before the judgment seat of Christ****, so that each one may be recompensed for his deeds in the body, according to what he has done, whether good or bad."* [200]

All of redeemed humanity will stand before the judgment seat of Jesus. They will be evaluated and *"recompensed"* (compensated, rewarded) according to the exercise, experiences and activities of their faith, or lack thereof, while on the earth. They will be compensated, whether they looked forward to the Messiah, through faith, while living during the Old Covenant, or they identified, through faith, with Jesus in His death, burial and resurrection while living during the New Covenant.

Paul gives us more insight into what will occur at the judgment seat of Christ, when he writes:

> *"According to the grace of God which was given to me, like a wise master builder I laid a foundation, and another is building on it. But* ***each man must be careful how he builds on it. For no man can lay a foundation other than the one which is laid, which is Jesus Christ.*** *Now if any man builds on the foundation with gold, silver, precious stones, wood, hay, straw,* ***each man's work will become evident;*** ***for the day will show it*** *because it is*

[200] 2Corinthians 5:9-10 NASB (emphasis mine)

*to be revealed with fire, and the fire itself **will test the quality** of each man's work. **If any man's work which he has built on it remains, he will receive a reward. If any man's work is burned up, he will suffer loss; but he himself will be saved,** yet so as through fire."* [201]

It is the *quality* of our life of faith that will be evaluated by Jesus. The *quality* of our rewards will be based on the results of this evaluation. We, as followers of Jesus, will not come under condemnation and enter into the judgment of God during our evaluation by Jesus. Our faith and redemption frees us from this condemnation and judgment. It is the quality of our works of faith that will be evaluated.

Earlier in the book I mentioned that Jesus lived His life with an expectation of reward. Jesus encouraged His disciples, and us, to live with this same expectation.[202] Jesus, along with Paul and other New Testament writers mention rewards that will be given to individuals as a result of their life of faith.[203] At the judgment seat of Jesus, we will receive rewards, garments and crowns, based on our obedience, actions and activities of faith while serving Him. These rewards will be ours and will remain with us throughout eternity. Some will receive more than others, based upon this evaluation by Jesus. Some may receive very little. Yet, even those who receive very little reward will enter into their regency responsibilities with the rest of righteous humanity, and will participate in the *Marriage Supper of the Lamb* and live within the new Jerusalem.

The Millennial Reign of Jesus & His Followers

There are many, many more characteristics that describe what the 1000-year reign of Jesus on the earth will be like – too numerous to go into any great detail, here. The earth will experience a tremendous renaissance and a dynamic restoration, as a result of the visible, complete Kingdom of God and the reign of Jesus coming to the earth. Here are a few of these characteristics:

---

[201] 1Corinthians 3:10-15 NASB (emphasis mine)

[202] Matthew 20:1-16; Matthew 25:19-23; Matthew 6:6; Revelation 22:12; Revelation 3:11;

[203] Luke 19:11-27; Colossians 3:23-24; Romans 2:6; James 1:12; Philippians 3:14; Hebrews 11:6; 1Corinthians 9:12; 2Timothy 4:7-8

- Creation experiences its liberation from the effects of sin, as a result of the glorification of the sons of God [204]
- The life-expectancy of mortal humanity living upon the earth is extended throughout this 1000-year period [205]
- Those humans who live into the 1000-year reign of Jesus will have the word of God and the gospel of the Kingdom of God declared to them, that they may believe and be born again through faith in Jesus [206]
- The peoples of the earth will stream to Jerusalem to learn the ways of God and to hear His word, from Jesus and His followers [207]
- The areas of the earth that were damaged or destroyed during the Tribulation period will be restored and rebuilt [208]

Throughout this 1000-year period of the reign of Jesus, those members of humanity who have not been physically resurrected will live and flourish upon the earth. They will continue to have children, who will grow up and have children of their own. The life-expectancy of these individuals will increase; living for several hundred years, or more. As a result, the population of the earth will increase and be restored after so many died resulting from the plagues, wars and judgments of God that occurred during the Tribulation period. During this 1000-year period, humanity will accomplish one of the conditions necessary to complete our divine mandate – to multiply and fill the earth. Still, physical death for mortal individuals will occur during this 1000-year period because they will be living in bodies that have been corrupted by sin and its results.

Righteousness will reign during these 1000 years as individuals willingly submit themselves to the reign of God, more and more. Active resistance and rebellious behavior will significantly decrease because there will be no direct temptation and opposition to the

---

[204] Isaiah 11:6-9;

[205] Isaiah 65:20-22

[206] Isaiah 66:18-19

[207] Isaiah 2:3

[208] Ezekiel 36:33-36

Kingdom of God. Satan will be held in prison and not actively deceiving and tempting mortal humanity. There will be occasional acts of lawlessness due to these individuals surrendering their wills to the sinful nature and desires of their minds and bodies, even as they learn the ways of God. The relationship between humanity, the creatures of the earth, and nature will be increasingly reconciled and restored, and humanity will not make war anymore:

> *"And the wolf will dwell with the lamb, and the leopard will lie down with the young goat, and the calf and the young lion and the fatling together; and a little boy will lead them. Also, the cow and the bear will graze, their young will lie down together, and the lion will eat straw like the ox. The nursing child will play by the hole of the cobra, and the weaned child will put his hand on the viper's den. They will not hurt or destroy in all My holy mountain, for the earth will be full of the knowledge of the LORD as the waters cover the sea."* [209]

> *"For the law will go forth from Zion and the word of the LORD from Jerusalem. And He will judge between the nations, and will render decisions for many peoples; and they will hammer their swords into plowshares and their spears into pruning hooks. Nation will not lift up sword against nation, and never again will they learn war."* [210]

There will be no direct temptation and seeds of rebellion sown in the hearts of mortal humanity because Satan will not be present and active upon the earth. Yet, at the end of this 1000 years, Satan will be released upon the earth, by God, for a short time. [211]

The Earth Is Completely Subdued

Throughout the history of fallen humanity, the Kingdom of God was "veiled" and only partially experienced as it confronted, engaged and interacted with humanity and the earth, prophetically, to accomplish God's will. Now, for 1,000 years, the Kingdom of God

---

[209] Isaiah 11:6-9 – NASB

[210] Isaiah 2:3-4 NASB

[211] Revelation 20:1-3

has been *visibly present* and active on the earth, through Jesus and His followers, where people can directly see, experience, openly respond to and interact with it.

Likewise, throughout this same period of fallen humanity, the domain of darkness was "veiled' and only partially experienced as it confronted, engaged and interacted with humanity and the earth, prophetically, to accomplish Satan's will. Now, following the 1,000-year reign of the Kingdom of God, Satan is released from his prison. He is now able to be *visibly present* and active on the earth, where people can see, experience and openly respond to and interact with him. Satan uses this visibility and direct interaction to personally recruit for and lead a final, direct attack against Jesus, His followers, and the Kingdom of God.

The book of Revelation tells us what happens in this final, direct confrontation between the Kingdom of God and Satan:

> *"When the thousand years are completed, Satan will be released from his prison, and will come out to deceive the nations which are in the four corners of the earth, Gog and Magog, to gather them together for the war; the number of them is like the sand of the seashore. And they came up on the broad plain of the earth and surrounded the camp of the saints and the beloved city, and fire came down from heaven and devoured them. And the devil who deceived them was thrown into the lake of fire and brimstone, where the beast and the false prophet are also; and they will be tormented day and night forever and ever."* [212]

By the end of this 1000-year period of Jesus' reign, humanity has multiplied and filled the earth – satisfying one of the requirements for completing their divine mandate. Yet, not all of these people are righteous and loyal to Jesus and the Kingdom of God. We see this when Satan leads an army of rebellious humanity – *"the number of them is like the sand of the seashore"*. Satan has deceived these people into believing that this rebellion against Jesus, His followers, and the Kingdom of God is a worthy cause and a winnable effort.

---

[212] Revelation 20:7-10 NASB (emphasis mine)

As Satan and this innumerable army from across the planet approaches *"the camp of the saints and the beloved city"*, the new Jerusalem, to engage and wage war against Jesus and immortal humanity, the Father, Himself, takes the battle into His own hands. From Heaven, He sends fire upon this vast army, destroying them. Finally, to bring God's complete judgment and sentence upon Satan for his rebellion, treason and sedition against Him and His Kingdom, Satan is completely defeated, subdued, and thrown into the Lake of Fire. There, he will suffer eternal torment and agony with the Antichrist and the False Prophet.

Humanity's Mandate Is Completed

Upon the completion of the 1,000-year reign, we see immortal humanity, led by Jesus, ruling the entire earth from the new Jerusalem. We see the earth and the natural, physical world set free from its bondage; no longer "groaning" from sin's effects. We see the cities and nations of the earth rebuilt and re-established after the Tribulation period. We see the animals of the earth living in harmony with one another and with humanity. We see the people of the earth desiring to know God and to learn more about the Kingdom of God. We see the Kingdom truths and realities spreading across the earth through the followers of Jesus, who communicate and demonstrate its realities. We see that mortal humanity has multiplied to the point of filling the earth. And, finally, we see the earth completely subdued, where the evil, rebellious elements that have filled the earth with their corrupting influences and activities have been removed, no longer to operate upon the earth.

Humanity has completed their great commission – their divine mandate. All of its conditions have been entirely satisfied. So, is this the end? Is there anything left in God's plan for humanity? Where do we go from here? Let's see what the Bible has to say about this.

The Destruction of the Corrupted & The Judgment of the Unredeemed

Paul tells us what happens once humanity's divine mandate is completed:

> *"For as in Adam all die, so also in Christ all will be made alive. But each in his own order:* **Christ the first fruits,** *after that* **those who are Christ's at His coming,** **then comes the end, when He hands over the kingdom to the God and Father,** **when He has abolished all rule and all authority and power.** *For* **He must reign** **until He has put all His enemies under His feet.** *The last enemy that will be abolished* **is death.** *For* HE HAS PUT ALL THINGS IN SUBJECTION UNDER HIS FEET. *But when He says, "All things are put in subjection," it is evident that He is excepted who put all things in subjection to Him.* **When all things are subjected to Him, then the Son Himself also will be subjected to the One who subjected all things to Him,** *so that God may be all in all."* [213]

Once righteous humanity completes their divine mandate, under the leadership of Jesus, Jesus subjects Himself to the Father by handing over the complete Kingdom rule of the earth, to the Father. This act of *willing* subjection completes the initial regency role and related activities that God gave humanity at their creation.

John, in the book of Revelation, expands on what Paul tells us about these final events that complete humanity's divine mandate, as well as what follows:

> *"Then I saw a great white throne and Him who sat upon it,* **from whose presence earth and heaven fled away, and no place was found for them.** *And* **I saw the dead, the great and the small, standing before the throne,** *and books were opened; and another book was opened, which is the book of life; and* **the dead were judged from the things which were written in the books, according to their deeds.** *And the sea gave up the dead which were in it, and* **death and Hades** *gave up the dead which were in them; and they were judged, every one of them according to their deeds. Then* **death and**

---

213 1Corinthians 15:22-28 NASB (emphasis mine)

Hades were thrown into the lake of fire. This is the second death, the lake of fire. And if anyone's name was not found written in the book of life, he was thrown into the lake of fire." [214]

Physical death became a reality in the human experience when Adam and Eve engaged in their rebellion against God in the Garden. When God placed them there and told them not to eat of the tree of the knowledge of good and evil, God warned them:

"You are free to eat from any tree in the garden; but you must not eat from the tree of the knowledge of good and evil, for when you eat from it you will certainly die." [215]

When God warned them not to eat from the tree, He literally told them, *"...for when you eat from it, in dying you will die"*. The punishment would be the experience of spiritual death and physical death. Their spiritual death, or relational separation from God, would bring about their, eventual, physical death. When unredeemed humanity physically dies, they go to a place called Hades or Hell, which is a holding place for the unrighteous dead to stay until the time of their judgment.

Therefore, the *dead* – those of humanity who were unrepentant and hostile toward God in their hearts when they physically died, will stand before the throne of God to give account for their activities while on the earth. They will be judged for their rebellion because they did not repent and identify with Jesus in His death, burial and resurrection, so as to be born again and saved from the wrath of God. They will be thrown into the Lake of Fire, where they will live and be tormented, forever. This is called the *second death*. They died once, and now they will live, again, within the Lake of Fire, separated from the presence and Kingdom of God, eternally. This is the second death – alive, yet dead.

Then, Death and Hades (Hell) will be thrown into the lake of fire. When unrighteous, rebellious humanity is judged before the throne of God, and the books are opened, Hades and physical death will no longer be needed or relevant. All of humanity, redeemed and

---

[214] Revelation 20:11-15 NASB (emphasis nine)
[215] Genesis 2:16-17 NASB (emphasis mine)

unredeemed, will no longer be subject to physical death. Unrighteous humanity will spend eternity in the lake of fire with Satan and his demonic forces, and righteous humanity will spend eternity on the new earth, with God (the Father, Son and Holy Spirit) and His angels.

We need to understand that Heaven is a temporary holding place for redeemed humanity. Once they return to the earth with Jesus, to begin the 1,000-year reign of the Kingdom of God, they will not return to Heaven. They will remain on the present earth and, then, on the new earth when it is created. What happens to the present earth and the heavens, including Heaven, where God resides? John sums it all up at the end of Revelation, when he is shown the final scene at the end of what is referred to as *"the first things"*:

> *"Then **I saw a new heaven and a new earth; for the first heaven and the first earth passed away,** and there is no longer any sea. And **I saw the holy city, new Jerusalem, coming down out of heaven from God,** made ready as a bride adorned for her husband. And I heard a loud voice from the throne, saying, "**Behold, the tabernacle of God is among men, and He will dwell among them, and they shall be His people, and God Himself will be among them,** and He will wipe away every tear from their eyes; **and there will no longer be any death;** there will no longer be any mourning, or crying, or pain; **the first things have passed away.**" And He who sits on the throne said, "**Behold, I am making all things new.**" And He said, "Write, for **these words are faithful and true.**" Then He said to me, "It is done. I am the Alpha and the Omega, the beginning and the end. I will give to the one who thirsts from the spring of the water of life without cost. **He who overcomes will inherit these things, and I will be his God and he will be My son.**".* [216]

The present heavens, including the place where God resides, and Earth will be destroyed. God and His throne will come down to the new earth, where He will dwell with His people, immortal humanity, forever. Why are the heavens and the earth destroyed? Because

---

[216] Revelation 21:1-7 – NASB (emphasis mine)

they have been corrupted by sin, evil and rebellion. The heavens have been corrupted in three ways:

1. By humanity, abandoning the remains (space/planetary junk) of their rebellious attempts to extend their rule beyond the earth – the domain assigned to them by God at their creation.[217]

2. By the presence and operation of demonic forces "in the heavenlies".[218]

3. By angelic rebellion - Heaven, the location of God and His throne, was corrupted by the rebellion of Lucifer (Satan) and his angels before humanity was ever placed on the earth.[219]

The End of the First Things

From what Paul tells us in 1Corinthians and John tells us in Revelation, the completion of humanity's divine mandate brings about the final judgments and activities relating to this age of "*first things*". Upon righteous humanity completing their great commission, we find:

- Sin, Hades/Hell, and Death are abolished
- All things on the earth are subjected to Jesus
- Jesus hands over the dominion of the earth to the Father
- Jesus subjects Himself to the Father
- The Father appears on His throne
- The current earth and heavens are removed; destroyed[220]
- Death and Hades give up the dead that are in them
- Sinful humanity stand before the throne of God and books are opened, including the book of life

---

[217] Psalm 89:11; Psalm 115:16

[218] Daniel 10:12-14; Ephesians 6:10-12

[219] Luke 10:18; Isaiah 14:12-15; Revelation 12:7-12

[220] 2Peter 3:7,10,12

- Sinful humanity is judged according to their deeds, which are written in the books
- Death and Hades/Hell are thrown into the lake of fire
- Those whose names do not appear in the book of life are thrown into the lake of fire – this is the second death
- There is a new heavens and a new earth
- The new Jerusalem descends a second time but this time to the new earth
- The Father, Himself, will be with His people, dwelling among them, forever
- There will no longer be any death, mourning, crying, or pain
- The *first things* are completed and gone – it is done!
- God makes all things new

The age of the *first things* is completed. The beginning of the *next things* has come:

> *"And He who sits on the throne said, "**Behold, I am making all things new.**" And He said, "Write, for **these words are faithful and true.**" Then He said to me, "**It is done.**""* [221]

- *Takeaways for the reader:*

  - When Jesus returns with His followers to rule the earth, they will with a rod of iron. They will defeat the Antichrist, False Prophet, and nations and armies of rebellious humanity upon their arrival, and will rule those humans that remain so as to subdue them, govern them, and instruct and lead them in the truths and realities of the Kingdom of God.
  - Upon the defeat of rebellious humanity and the establishment of the Kingdom of God on the earth, the

---

[221] Revelation 21:5-6 NASB (emphasis mine)

New Jerusalem will descend from heaven to the earth. This is where Jesus and His redeemed followers will live during the 1,000-year reign, as well as when the new earth is created.

- o The Judgment Seat of Christ and the Marriage Supper of the Lamb will take place on the earth after the Kingdom of God is established. All of righteous humanity will be together with Jesus and these events and activities will begin the 1,000-year reign of Jesus and His followers.

- o The earth is completely subdued at the end of the 1,000 years reign and humanity has completed their divine mandate. Jesus, as Lord, King and leader of all humanity, subjects Himself to the Father, representing all of humanity, submitting and presenting the dominion and the rule of the earth back to the Father.

- o Satan and sinful humanity are judged and thrown into the Lake of Fire, forever. The present heavens and earth are destroyed, and a new heavens and earth are created. God's throne descends to the new earth and He dwells with immortal humanity forever. This is the end of *the first things*.

- • *Small group questions*:

  - o When Jesus and we return to the earth to establish the Kingdom of God, we will rule with righteousness, justice, peace, and a rod of iron. What does this tell us about the nature and character of God and His Kingdom? What does it tell us about ourselves, as Jesus' followers and God's image bearers and regents?

  - o To we return to subdue the earth, we must subdue rebellious humanity. What do you think about that? What are the implications of that? Does that make a difference to us as to how we live and conduct ourselves, now, as Jesus' followers and image bearers to the people around us?

- As those who will rule with Jesus upon the earth during the 1,000-year reign, we will rule based upon the rewards we receive for our deeds of faith we engage in now. We determine our rewards based upon our faith activities in this life. What does that mean for us, now? How can we grow in our proportion of faith, so we receive the rewards God has in store for us?

- Discuss the New Jerusalem, what it is, what it does, and what it means to us as followers of Jesus. What is your response to these images and descriptions, as given to us by John in Revelation? What impact does that have upon you now?

- Discuss the Lake of Fire, what it does, who is there, and what it means. What is your response to these images and descriptions? What impact does that have upon you now?

- The *first things* will be completed. What are the *next things* the Bible tells us about and what does that say and mean to us?

MOVING FORWARD - WHAT IS NEXT?

As I said at the beginning, in my *Author's Note*, this book is a training manual. It is intended to:

- establish the scriptural and theological premise that humanity must complete their great commission, a specific mandate that God gave us at our creation, if we are to move forward with His eternal plan for us
- lay the scriptural foundation for this mandate and that God has been and continues to work in and with humanity to bring about the completion of it.

This book is a high-level introduction to this reality. As a result, there is much more to be said concerning the topics introduced and discussed here. As followers of Jesus and those who are responsible to ultimately complete this mandate, under Jesus' leadership, we must delve into these topics to a greater degree, as individuals and faith communities, to understand our responsibilities and God's expectations for us in this *passionate pursuit*.

We must discover how to practically engage with God in His prophetic training. We must recognize and embrace what He desires to accomplish with it, in our generation. We must recognize and embrace what this will look like and how we should respond to the Holy Spirit as He prophetically invites, instructs, trains and mentors us, individually and as faith communities. As we will discover, this process will take some time. Yet, if we willingly and faithfully engage and cooperate with God, we can, as the children of Israel did in the wilderness, accomplish what He desires in a relatively short period of time; perhaps, within a single generation.

To effectively prepare us to complete this mandate, God has given us:

- a prophetic training manual containing His Kingdom truths, realities and activities (the Bible)

- a Master Teacher and Mentor (the Holy Spirit)
- a visible, complete example (Jesus) of what God is working to accomplish in and through us; His Kingdom people
- ascension gifts from Jesus who are to specifically equip us for service to the Kingdom of God, and to build us up to the proportion of faith necessary to engage and cooperate with Him in His prophetic Kingdom activities
- generational elders (mentors) who will come along side individuals and faith communities to coach, train and mentor in these spiritual truths, realities and prophetic activities

We briefly introduced many of these spiritual realities in this book. Yet, in order to make them practical and workable within our faith experience with God, it is necessary to go into greater depth and bring greater clarity and understanding to them. To accomplish this, I am preparing another book – another training manual to help make these spiritual realities and activities easier for us to grasp, implement and integrate. As with this book, it will be intended for small groups, training environments and mentoring relationships.

There is much that God wants to accomplish in and through our generation, and He has implemented a prophetic training that will help us to make significant progress in our efforts to complete humanity's divine mandate. He is looking for those who recognize this and are willing to engage with Him as active, willing participants with the Holy Spirit. As we will discover even more, the Holy Spirit, the Spirit of Christ, is the most important Person and the most important relationship we have in this world. For, "*apart from Him, we can do nothing*".

ABOUT THE AUTHOR

Tom has been a follower of Jesus for nearly 50 years. He graduated from the University of Missouri in St. Louis with a Bachelor of Science degree in Business Administration. Tom also received his Master of Arts degree in Practical Theology from the Regent University School of Divinity in Virginia Beach, Virginia. Tom and his wife, Andrea, reside in the St. Louis, Missouri area.

In addition to *"Our Divine Mandate"*, Tom has written the book *"Studies In The Kingdom Of God"*, which is also available through Amazon.

Tom can be contacted at: *tcasey.stl@gmail.com*

NOTES

NOTES

Made in the USA
Las Vegas, NV
14 June 2021